Presented to

_____

Date

_____

By

_____

Promises from God for Men of Color

Copyright ©2021

Published By:
Urban Spirit! Publishing Company LLC.
753 Walden Blvd. Atlanta, GA 30349

Scripture Quotations are taken from the Holy Bible King James Version
Some material has been Taken from the *Men of Color Study Bible* copyright ©2001 Nia Publishing Co. Inc.

Urban Spirit! Publishing Co. LLC is an African American owned company based in Atlanta, GA. Started in 1993 by Mel Banks II, former Marketing director for Urban Ministries, Inc.

ALL Rights Reserved. No Portion of this Publication may be reproduced, stored in a Retrieval system, or transmitted in any form, by any means, electronic, mechanical, photocopy, recording, or otherwise without the expressed written consent of the Publisher. Urban Spirit! Publishing Co. LLC.

Produced by Urban Spirit! Publishing Co. LLC Project Staff:
Owner: Mel Banks II
Project Manager: Cheryl Wilson
Interior and cover design: Larry Taylor

PROMISES FROM GOD FOR
MEN OF COLOR

TABLE OF CONTENTS
The Christian Life

Commitment to Community	12
Armor of God	14
Belief	16
Commitment	18
Confidence	20
Courage	22
Discernment	24
Faith	26
Faithfulness	28
Forgiveness - The Doorway to Healing & Reconciliation	30
Forgiveness	32
Forgiveness - God's Extended Mercy	34
Generosity	36
Gentleness	40
Goodness	42
Grace	44
Growth	46
Hope	48
Hope for the Future	50
Joy	52
Kindness	54
Knowing God	56
Leadership	58
Love	60
Patience	62
Peace	64

Perseverance 66
Prayer... 68
Prayer... 70
Prayer Life 72
Prayer & Salvation 74
Purpose 76
Reliance 78
Salvation... 80
Self-Confidence 82
Self-Control... 84
Ministry... 86
Serving 88
Suffering... 90
Trusting 92
Witnessing 94

Family/Parenting Issues

Children 98
Discipline 100
Discipline 102
Gift of Children 104
God as Example 106
Marriage 108
Fatherhood 110
Responsibility of Parenting 112
Teaching Children 114

Attributes of God

Authority 118
Forgiveness... 120
Holy 122

Justice 124
Love 126
Love 128
Mercy 130
Omniscience.. 132
Patience... 134
Presence.. 136
Provision 138
Protection... 140
Righteousness 142
Sovereignty 144
Truth 146

Relationship Issues

Aging 150
Community 152
Elderly 154
Friendship... 156
Friendship... 158
Intimacy with Others....................................... 160
Love for Others 162
Restoration 164
Brotherhood.. 166
Unity of Believers 168

What the Bible Says About

Anger... 172
Beauty... 174
Busyness.. 176
Positive Thinking 178
Confidence 180
Giving.. 182

Guidance	184
Knowing God's Will	186
Leadership - Brick by Brick Together	188
Leadership	190
National Heritage	192
Security	194
Self - Worth	196
Singleness	198
Single Life	200
Suffering	202
Thoughts	204
Truth	206
Vanity	208
Words We Say	210

Trials and Troubles

Brokenness	214
Death	216
Despair	218
Discouragement	220
Fear	222
Grief	224
Loneliness	226
Sorrow	228
Stress	230
Temptation	232
Trouble	234
Positive Thinking	236
Worry	238

1 CORINTHIANS 6:19-20

NEW INTERNATIONAL VERSION (NIV)

James K. Bennett

[19] Do you not know that your bodies are temples of the Holy Spirit, who is in you, whom you have received from God? You are not your own; [20] you were bought at a price. Therefore honor God with your bodies.

When thinking about disease prevention, think about the true meaning of health. Health is not just the absence of disease, but also physical wellbeing: keeping your body, mind, and spirit strong and healthy for evangelizing. It is important to be concerned about your physical well-being. This could be as simple as drinking a glass of water, taking a morning run, completing your annual physical, reading a book, or ensuring that you don't let stress take over your life. Whatever concern you may have, your body is one of the first few gifts that the Lord entrusted to you as your responsibility. Christian men should be aware of what great care God put into the design of the human body and the immense wealth that went into the creation of their temple. Upholding health, preventing disease, and preserving wellness of the body is a critical, yet often overlooked, part of being a devoted follower of Christ. As men, we often neglect going to the doctor for various reasons, but it is frequently forgotten that maintaining a healthy body is key duty of the Christian man. How can you fulfill your duty as the head of your household, as Christ is the head of the church, if you do not take care of your temple? You must consider your bodies as the temple of God. Reflect on what you put in your body, letting your body relax and renew, and explore fun and unique ways to keep your body active. This can be accomplished through proper nutrition, exercise, and education. Therefore as you continue to be inspired by the words of those before us, continue to encourage one another to honor God by maintaining a healthy body, mind, and soul. Equally as each of you has been provided your body as a gift, continue to use it in the manner in which the Lord continues to bless you abundantly, many times over.

> *"Knowledge is power and with screening, detection, and education, knowledge is life!"*

James K. Bennett, M.D. F.A.C.S. CEO, *Midtown Urology and Midtown Urology Surgical Center Adjunct Professor, Clark Atlanta University Adjunct Clinical Professor, Morehouse School of Medicine Clinical Assistant Professor, Emory University School of Medicine Atlanta, GA*

THE CHRISTIAN LIFE

COMMITMENT TO COMMUNITY

Rev. Floyd H. Flake

> *"And the Lord God took the man, and put him into the garden of Eden to dress it and to keep it"*
> (Gen. 2:15).

The creation of Adam and Eve is the beginning of family and community. Their community was the Garden of Eden, and they were charged with the responsibility of dressing and keeping it. Although God had provided everything that they needed to survive in the Garden, their future production was dependent upon their willingness to work, cultivate, nurture, and tend to it.

God gave Adam and Eve water, vegetables, fruits, herbs, gold and jewel stones, the treeof life, and enough knowledge to sustain them. However, they had to work in order to maintain and develop the garden to support themselves, and the land outside the garden

As I survey the world and see so many deteriorating and decaying communities, it is obvious that we have not nurtured and developed the communities that God has given us. These communities have an appreciating commodity called land, which should and could be more productive. When taken care of, this land is an appreciating asset, yet, we fail to build upon what we have been given by God.

God is calling on the Church to commit itself to community development so that the wonderful gift of community can once again be a productive place.

ARMOR OF GOD

Ephes. 6:13-18

Wherefore take unto you the whole armour of God, that ye may be able to withstand in the evil day, and having done all, to stand. Stand therefore, having your loins girt about with truth, and having on the breastplate of righteousness; And your feet shod with the preparation of the gospel of peace; Above all, taking the shield of faith, wherewith ye shall be able to quench all the fiery darts of the wicked. And take the helmet of salvation, and the sword of the Spirit, which is the word of God: Praying always with all prayer and supplication in the Spirit, and watching thereunto with all perseverance and supplication for all saints;

2 Cor. 10:4

(For the weapons of our warfare are not carnal, but mighty through God to the pulling down of strong holds;)

Hebrews 4:12

For the word of God is quick, and powerful, and sharper than any twoedged sword, piercing even to the dividing asunder of soul and spirit, and of the joints and marrow, and is a discerner of the thoughts and intents of the heart.

BELIEF

Jeremiah 33:3
Call unto me, and I will answer thee, and shew thee great and mighty things, which thou knowest not.

Mark 11:24
Therefore I say unto you, What things soever ye desire, when ye pray, believe that ye receive them, and ye shall have them.

John 14:13-14
And whatsoever ye shall ask in my name, that will I do, that the Father may be glorified in the Son. If ye shall ask any thing in my name, I will do it.

2 Peter 1:3-4
According as his divine power hath given unto us all things that pertain unto life and godliness, through the knowledge of him that hath called us to glory and virtue: Whereby are given unto us exceeding great and precious promises: that by these ye might be partakers of the divine nature, having escaped the corruption that is in the world through lust.

Jude 1:20
But ye, beloved, building up yourselves on your most holy faith, praying in the Holy Ghost

It always seems impossible until it is done."
Nelson Mandela

COMMITMENT

1 Kings 8:61
Let your heart therefore be perfect with the Lord our God, to walk in his statutes, and to keep his commandments, as at this day.

Proverbs 16:3
Commit thy works unto the Lord, and thy thoughts shall be established.

Mark 8:34
And when he had called the people unto him with his disciples also, he said unto them, Whosoever will come after me, let him deny himself, and take up his cross, and follow me.

Luke 14:27
And whosoever doth not bear his cross, and come after me, cannot be my disciple.

Romans 12:1-2
I beseech you therefore, brethren, by the mercies of God, that ye present your bodies a living sacrifice, holy, acceptable unto God, which is your reasonable service. And be not conformed to this world: but be ye transformed by the renewing of your mind, that ye may prove what is that good, and acceptable, and perfect, will of God.

Psalm 27:1-3
The Lord is my light and my salvation; whom shall I fear? the Lord is the strength of my life; of whom shall I be afraid? When the wicked, even mine enemies and my foes, came upon me to eat up my flesh, they stumbled and fell. Though an host should encamp against me, my heart shall not fear: though war should rise against me, in this will I be confident.

Isaiah 32:17
And the work of righteousness shall be peace; and the effect of righteousness quietness and assurance for ever.

Hebrews 4:16
Let us therefore come boldly unto the throne of grace, that we may obtain mercy, and find grace to help in time of need.

Hebrews 13:6
So that we may boldly say, The Lord is my helper, and I will not fear what man shall do unto me.

1 John 5:14
And this is the confidence that we have in him, that, if we ask any thing according to his will, he heareth us:

Have a vision. Be demanding.
Colin Powell,

One important key to success is self-confidence. An important key to self-confidence is preparation.
Arthur Ashe

COURAGE

Psalm 18:29
For by thee I have run through a troop; and by my God have I leaped over a wall.

Psalm 27:14
Wait on the Lord: be of good courage, and he shall strengthen thine heart: wait, I say, on the Lord.

Psalm 31:24
Be of good courage, and he shall strengthen your heart, all ye that hope in the Lord.

Isaiah 43:2-3
When thou passest through the waters, I will be with thee; and through the rivers, they shall not overflow thee: when thou walkest through the fire, thou shalt not be burned; neither shall the flame kindle upon thee. For I am the Lord thy God, the Holy One of Israel, thy Saviour: I gave Egypt for thy ransom, Ethiopia and Seba for thee.

Isaiah 50:7
For the Lord God will help me; therefore shall I not be confounded: therefore have I set my face like a flint, and I know that I shall not be ashamed.

DISCERNMENT

J. Thompson

The gift of discernment is best epitomized in the life of Jesus Christ. He was able to discern the thoughts and hearts of those whom He encountered (Matt. 12:25, John 6:6). The gift of discernment allows one to see beyond words and actions in order to uncover hidden motivations and intent (Prov. 16:9). Because discernment is a gift from God, it is always subject to the written revelation of God—the Word of God.

John 16:13

Howbeit when he, the Spirit of truth, is come, he will guide you into all truth: for he shall not speak of himself; but whatsoever he shall hear, that shall he speak: and he will shew you things to come.

1 Cor. 2:14-16

But the natural man receiveth not the things of the Spirit of God: for they are foolishness unto him: neither can he know them, because they are spiritually discerned. But he that is spiritual judgeth all things, yet he himself is judged of no man. For who hath known the mind of the Lord, that he may instruct him? But we have the mind of Christ.

2 Tim. 2:7

Consider what I say; and the Lord give thee understanding in all things.

1 John 4:1

Beloved, believe not every spirit, but try the spirits whether they are of God: because many false prophets are gone out into the world.

1 John 4:6

We are of God: he that knoweth God heareth us; he that is not of God heareth not us. Hereby know we the spirit of truth, and the spirit of error.

FAITH

Hebrews 11:1
Now faith is the substance of things hoped for, the evidence of things not seen.

Isaiah 40:31
But they that wait upon the Lord shall renew their strength; they shall mount up with wings as eagles; they shall run, and not be weary; and they shall walk, and not faint.

John 14:12
Verily, verily, I say unto you, He that believeth on me, the works that I do shall he do also; and greater works than these shall he do; because I go unto my Father.

Romans 4:3
For what saith the scripture? Abraham believed God, and it was counted unto him for righteousness.

1 Peter 1:8
Whom having not seen, ye love; in whom, though now ye see him not, yet believing, ye rejoice with joy unspeakable and full of glory:

FAITHFULNESS

Psalm 37:5

Commit thy way unto the Lord; trust also in him; and he shall bring it to pass.

Psalm 37:28

For the Lord loveth judgment, and forsaketh not his saints; they are preserved for ever: but the seed of the wicked shall be cut off.

Proverbs 2:7-8

He layeth up sound wisdom for the righteous: he is a buckler to them that walk uprightly. He keepeth the paths of judgment, and preserveth the way of his saints.

Proverbs 3:3-4

Let not mercy and truth forsake thee: bind them about thy neck; write them upon the table of thine heart: So shalt thou find favour and good understanding in the sight of God and man.

Rev. 2:10

Fear none of those things which thou shalt suffer: behold, the devil shall cast some of you into prison, that ye may be tried; and ye shall have tribulation ten days: be thou faithful unto death, and I will give thee a crown of life.

FORGIVENESS:

The Doorway to Healing & Reconciliation

Willard Ashley Sr.

What do you do when someone hurts you? What thoughts go through your mind when someone makes you angry? Under what circumstances are you willing to forgive? What are the limits to your ability to forgive?

How do you forgive the partner who cheated on you? How do you forgive those who abandoned you? How do you forgive yourself for the sins, failures, missed opportunities, and inconsistencies found in every life? How do you forgive the drunk driver who killed your loved one? How do you forgive the boss that fired you or down sized you?

Forgiveness is divine. It is the take-home exam in the Christian curriculum. Forgiveness is the measure of your walk with God. To forgive takes character, vision, and strength. It is a spiritually mature attitude that releases those who have wounded you from threat of your wrath. Forgiveness opens the door to healing and reconciliation. To forgive is the first step toward ending the cycle of pain. It is your declaration of independence from the notion to get even. Forgiveness is your decision move from victim to victor. Forgiveness is the heart specialist that repairs our broken hearts and damaged relationships. Forgiveness is of God.

FORGIVENESS

Matthew 6:14-15
  For if ye forgive men their trespasses, your heavenly Father will also forgive you: But if ye forgive not men their trespasses, neither will your Father forgive your trespasses.

Luke 17:3-4
  Take heed to yourselves: If thy brother trespass against thee, rebuke him; and if he repent, forgive him. And if he trespass against thee seven times in a day, and seven times in a day turn again to thee, saying, I repent; thou shalt forgive him.

Romans 5:10-11
  For if, when we were enemies, we were reconciled to God by the death of his Son, much more, being reconciled, we shall be saved by his life. And not only so, but we also joy in God through our Lord Jesus Christ, by whom we have now received the atonement.

Matthew 18:21-22
  Then came Peter to him, and said, Lord, how oft shall my brother sin against me, and I forgive him? till seven times? Jesus saith unto him, I say not unto thee, Until seven times: but, Until seventy times seven.

Col. 3:13
  Forbearing one another, and forgiving one another, if any man have a quarrel against any: even as Christ forgave you, so also do ye.

FORGIVENESS:
God's Extended Mercy
Pastor Philip L. Rodman

Are you having trouble forgiving someone who has hurt you? Perhaps you are holding a grudge, or you are upset about something they have done to you. You have even uttered the words:

"I can't forgive them because you don't understand what they have put me through."

When we step back and take an account of how often we have offended God, and yet He still forgives us, we cannot possibly say that we will not forgive others. In fact, Jesus says that God will turn us over to the tormentors "if ye from your hearts forgive not every one his brother their trespasses" (Matt. 18:35).

God extends His mercy to us even when we do not deserve it. He realizes that we are human, subject to frailties and weaknesses that often degrade our usefulness to Him. Yet, God's Word says, "If we confess our sins, he is faithful and just to forgive us our sins, and to cleanse us from all unrighteousness" (1 John 1:9). God clearly tells you that if He can forgive you, then you must be willing to forgive others.

God's mercy is evident to us. The Bible says they are new every morning (Lam. 3:23).

Having trouble forgiving others? Remember that God has forgiven us. That is enough to make us want to extend the same to even our worst offender!

GENEROSITY

Proverbs 11:25
The liberal soul shall be made fat: and he that watereth shall be watered also himself.

Luke 6:30
Give to every man that asketh of thee; and of him that taketh away thy goods ask them not again.

Luke 6:38
Give, and it shall be given unto you; good measure, pressed down, and shaken together, and running over, shall men give into your bosom. For with the same measure that ye mete withal it shall be measured to you again.

2 Cor. 9:6-7
But this I say, He which soweth sparingly shall reap also sparingly; and he which soweth bountifully shall reap also bountifully. Every man according as he purposeth in his heart, so let him give; not grudgingly, or of necessity: for God loveth a cheerful giver.

> *"The highest test of the civilization of any race is in its willingness to extend a helping hand to the less fortunate."*
>
> Booker T. Washington

GENTLENESS

Matthew 11:29
Take my yoke upon you, and learn of me; for I am meek and lowly in heart: and ye shall find rest unto your souls.

Ephes. 4:1-3
I therefore, the prisoner of the Lord, beseech you that ye walk worthy of the vocation wherewith ye are called, with all lowliness and meekness, with longsuffering, forbearing one another in love; Endeavouring to keep the unity of the Spirit in the bond of peace.

1 Tim. 6:11
But thou, O man of God, flee these things; and follow after righteousness, godliness, faith, love, patience, meekness.

Philip. 4:5
Let your moderation be known unto all men. The Lord is at hand.

1 Peter 3:3-4
Whose adorning let it not be that outward adorning of plaiting the hair, and of wearing of gold, or of putting on of apparel; But let it be the hidden man of the heart, in that which is not corruptible, even the ornament of a meek and quiet spirit, which is in the sight of God of great price.

GOODNESS

Matthew 5:13-16

Ye are the salt of the earth: but if the salt have lost his savour, wherewith shall it be salted? it is thenceforth good for nothing, but to be cast out, and to be trodden under foot of men. Ye are the light of the world. A city that is set on an hill cannot be hid. Neither do men light a candle, and put it under a bushel, but on a candlestick; and it giveth light unto all that are in the house. Let your light so shine before men, that they may see your good works, and glorify your Father which is in heaven.

Galatians 6:9

And let us not be weary in well doing: for in due season we shall reap, if we faint not.

Ephes. 2:10

For we are his workmanship, created in Christ Jesus unto good works, which God hath before ordained that we should walk in them.

James 3:13

Who is a wise man and endued with knowledge among you? let him shew out of a good conversation his works with meekness of wisdom.

3 John 1:11

Beloved, follow not that which is evil, but that which is good. He that doeth good is of God: but he that doeth evil hath not seen God.

GRACE

Psalm 116:5
Gracious is the Lord, and righteous; yea, our God is merciful.

Romans 5:1-2
Therefore being justified by faith, we have peace with God through our Lord Jesus Christ: By whom also we have access by faith into this grace wherein we stand, and rejoice in hope of the glory of God.

2 Cor. 8:9
For ye know the grace of our Lord Jesus Christ, that, though he was rich, yet for your sakes he became poor, that ye through his poverty might be rich.

2 Cor. 9:8
And God is able to make all grace abound toward you; that ye, always having all sufficiency in all things, may abound to every good work.

GROWTH

Psalm 119:105
Thy word is a lamp unto my feet, and a light unto my path.

Isaiah 30:21
And thine ears shall hear a word behind thee, saying, This is the way, walk ye in it, when ye turn to the right hand, and when ye turn to the left.

Proverbs 4:18
But the path of the just is as the shining light, that shineth more and more unto the perfect day.

Philip. 1:9
And this I pray, that your love may abound yet more and more in knowledge and in all judgment;

1 Tim. 4:15
Meditate upon these things; give thyself wholly to them; that thy profiting may appear to all.

HOPE

Psalm 147:11

The Lord taketh pleasure in them that fear him, in those that hope in his mercy.

Lament. 3:21-22

This I recall to my mind, therefore have I hope.

It is of the Lord's mercies that we are not consumed, because his compassions fail not.

Matthew 28:20

Teaching them to observe all things whatsoever I have commanded you: and, lo, I am with you alway, even unto the end of the world. Amen.

Hebrews 4:14-16

Seeing then that we have a great high priest, that is passed into the heavens, Jesus the Son of God, let us hold fast our profession. For we have not an high priest which cannot be touched with the feeling of our infirmities; but was in all points tempted like as we are, yet without sin. Let us therefore come boldly unto the throne of grace, that we may obtain mercy, and find grace to help in time of need.

Hebrews 13:5

Let your conversation be without covetousness; and be content with such things as ye have: for he hath said, I will never leave thee, nor forsake thee.

Proverbs 24:14
So shall the knowledge of wisdom be unto thy soul: when thou hast found it, then there shall be a reward, and thy expectation shall not be cut off.

Isaiah 40:31
But they that wait upon the Lord shall renew their strength; they shall mount up with wings as eagles; they shall run, and not be weary; and they shall walk, and not faint.

Jeremiah 29:11
For I know the thoughts that I think toward you, saith the Lord, thoughts of peace, and not of evil, to give you an expected end.

Luke 1:50
And his mercy is on them that fear him from generation to generation.

1 Peter 2:9
But ye are a chosen generation, a royal priesthood, an holy nation, a peculiar people; that ye should shew forth the praises of him who hath called you out of darkness into his marvellous light.

"Change will not come if we wait for some other person or some other time. We are the ones we've been waiting for. We are the change that we seek."

President Barack Obama

JOY

Psalm 5:11

But let all those that put their trust in thee rejoice: let them ever shout for joy, because thou defendest them: let them also that love thy name be joyful in thee.

Psalm 32:11

Be glad in the Lord, and rejoice, ye righteous: and shout for joy, all ye that are upright in heart.

Psalm 30:11-12

Thou hast turned for me my mourning into dancing: thou hast put off my sackcloth, and girded me with gladness; To the end that my glory may sing praise to thee, and not be silent. O Lord my God, I will give thanks unto thee for ever.

Psalm 92:4

For thou, Lord, hast made me glad through thy work: I will triumph in the works of thy hands.

James 1:2-3

My brethren, count it all joy when ye fall into divers temptations; Knowing this, that the trying of your faith worketh patience.

KINDNESS

Proverbs 11:16
A gracious woman retaineth honour: and strong men retain riches.

Proverbs 14:31
He that oppresseth the poor reproacheth his Maker: but he that honoureth him hath mercy on the poor.

> "The only justification for ever looking down on somebody is to pick them up."
> Jesse Jackson

Matthew 7:12
Therefore all things whatsoever ye would that men should do to you, do ye even so to them: for this is the law and the prophets.

1 Thes. 5:15
See that none render evil for evil unto any man; but ever follow that which is good, both among yourselves, and to all men.

2 Peter 1:5-7
And beside this, giving all diligence, add to your faith virtue; and to virtue knowledge; And to knowledge temperance; and to temperance patience; and to patience godliness; And to godliness brotherly kindness; and to brotherly kindness charity.

KNOWING GOD

Deut. 6:5
And thou shalt love the Lord thy God with all thine heart, and with all thy soul, and with all thy might.

Psalm 16:11
Thou wilt shew me the path of life: in thy presence is fulness of joy; at thy right hand there are pleasures for evermore.

Psalm 33:18
Behold, the eye of the Lord is upon them that fear him, upon them that hope in his mercy;

Psalm 34:15
The eyes of the Lord are upon the righteous, and his ears are open unto their cry.

Philip. 1:6
Being confident of this very thing, that he which hath begun a good work in you will perform it until the day of Jesus Christ:

LEADERSHIP

Proverbs 3:27
Withhold not good from them to whom it is due, when it is in the power of thine hand to do it.

Proverbs 15:22
Without counsel purposes are disappointed: but in the multitude of counsellors they are established.

Luke 17:10
So likewise ye, when ye shall have done all those things which are commanded you, say, We are unprofitable servants: we have done that which was our duty to do.

Ephes. 6:7
With good will doing service, as to the Lord, and not to men:

1 Peter 4:11
If any man speak, let him speak as the oracles of God; if any man minister, let him do it as of the ability which God giveth: that God in all things may be glorified through Jesus Christ, to whom be praise and dominion for ever and ever. Amen.

"A genuine leader is not a searcher for consensus but a molder of consensus."
Martin Luther King, Jr.

LOVE

Psalm 107:8-9

Oh that men would praise the Lord for his goodness, and for his wonderful works to the children of men! For he satisfieth the longing soul, and filleth the hungry soul with goodness.

Psalm 145:8

The Lord is gracious, and full of compassion; slow to anger, and of great mercy.

Isaiah 54:10

For the mountains shall depart, and the hills be removed; but my kindness shall not depart from thee, neither shall the covenant of my peace be removed, saith the Lord that hath mercy on thee.

Jeremiah 31:3

The Lord hath appeared of old unto me, saying, Yea, I have loved thee with an everlasting love: therefore with lovingkindness have I drawn thee.

1 Cor. 13:4-7

Charity suffereth long, and is kind; charity envieth not; charity vaunteth not itself, is not puffed up, Doth not behave itself unseemly, seeketh not her own, is not easily provoked, thinketh no evil; Rejoiceth not in iniquity, but rejoiceth in the truth; Beareth all things, believeth all things, hopeth all things, endureth all things.

"Hatred paralyzes life; love releases it. Hatred confuses life; love harmonizes it. Hatred darkens life; love illuminates it."

Martin Luther King, Jr.

PATIENCE

Psalm 37:7
Rest in the Lord, and wait patiently for him: fret not thyself because of him who prospereth in his way, because of the man who bringeth wicked devices to pass.

Psalm 86:15
But thou, O Lord, art a God full of compassion, and gracious, longsuffering, and plenteous in mercy and truth.

Psalm 130:5-6
I wait for the Lord, my soul doth wait, and in his word do I hope. My soul waiteth for the Lord more than they that watch for the morning: I say, more than they that watch for the morning.

Romans 5:3-5
And not only so, but we glory in tribulations also: knowing that tribulation worketh patience; And patience, experience; and experience, hope: And hope maketh not ashamed; because the love of God is shed abroad in our hearts by the Holy Ghost which is given unto us.

Galatians 5:22-23
But the fruit of the Spirit is love, joy, peace, longsuffering, gentleness, goodness, faith, Meekness, temperance: against such there is no law.

Patience is the key which solves all problems.
African proverb

PEACE

Psalm 119:165
Great peace have they which love thy law: and nothing shall offend them.

Isaiah 26:3
Thou wilt keep him in perfect peace, whose mind is stayed on thee: because he trusteth in thee.

Romans 8:6
For to be carnally minded is death; but to be spiritually minded is life and peace.

John 14:27
Peace I leave with you, my peace I give unto you: not as the world giveth, give I unto you. Let not your heart be troubled, neither let it be afraid.

Philip. 4:7
And the peace of God, which passeth all understanding, shall keep your hearts and minds through Christ Jesus.

PERSEVERANCE

Psalm 17:5
Hold up my goings in thy paths, that my footsteps slip not.

Romans 2:7
To them who by patient continuance in well doing seek for glory and honour and immortality, eternal life.

Galatians 6:9
And let us not be weary in well doing: for in due season we shall reap, if we faint not.

James 1:4-5
But let patience have her perfect work, that ye may be perfect and entire, wanting nothing. If any of you lack wisdom, let him ask of God, that giveth to all men liberally, and upbraideth not; and it shall be given him.

2 Cor. 1:20
For all the promises of God in him are yea, and in him Amen, unto the glory of God by us.

If you are going to achieve excellence in big things, you develop the habit in little matters. Excellence is not an exception, it is a prevailing attitude.

Colin Powell

PRAYER

Pastor Philip L. Rodman

One of the strongest weapons men have today is prayer. The Bible says that we must "pray without ceasing" (1 Thessalonians 5:17). The word "prayer" has so many meanings, including giving God thanks, confession of sins, worship, adoration, petitions (or supplication), and praise.

In the Book of Acts, Cornelius is described as a devout man. Why? Because he feared God, and he prayed! One day, as Cornelius was praying, he saw an angel appearing before him. When the angel saw Cornelius, he told him that his prayers had come up to God for a memorial before the Lord (see Acts 10:1-4). Cornelius was in need of a personal relationship with God and because he prayed, he got just what he wanted!

Why are some men reluctant to pray? Why doesn't prayer seem to be important in our lives? Could it be that we don't understand that prayer changes us more than it changes God? The Bible says that we are being conformed to the image of our Lord and Savior Jesus Christ (Romans 8:29). As we pray, we begin to line up our wishes and our petitions with what God wants for us as well as for those for whom we pray.

God wants to use us as, "vessels of honor . . . suitable for His use" (see 2 Timothy 2:21) in praying for those who may not be able to pray for themselves. As men of God, let's take the initiative to be prayer warriors for God. Let's take hold of God's altar and bring our petitions and the concerns of others to Him, and watch what happens.

PRAYER

Matthew 11:28-30
Come unto me, all ye that labour and are heavy laden, and I will give you rest. Take my yoke upon you, and learn of me; for I am meek and lowly in heart: and ye shall find rest unto your souls. For my yoke is easy, and my burden is light.

Matthew 26:41
Watch and pray, that ye enter not into temptation: the spirit indeed is willing, but the flesh is weak.

Ephes. 6:18
Praying always with all prayer and supplication in the Spirit, and watching thereunto with all perseverance and supplication for all saints;

Col. 4:2
Continue in prayer, and watch in the same with thanksgiving;

1 Thes. 5:16-18
Rejoice evermore. Pray without ceasing. In every thing give thanks: for this is the will of God in Christ Jesus concerning you.

PRAYER LIFE

Psalm 18:6

In my distress I called upon the Lord, and cried unto my God: he heard my voice out of his temple, and my cry came before him, even into his ears.

Matthew 6:25-28

Therefore I say unto you, Take no thought for your life, what ye shall eat, or what ye shall drink; nor yet for your body, what ye shall put on. Is not the life more than meat, and the body than raiment? Behold the fowls of the air: for they sow not, neither do they reap, nor gather into barns; yet your heavenly Father feedeth them. Are ye not much better than they? Which of you by taking thought can add one cubit unto his stature? And why take ye thought for raiment? Consider the lilies of the field, how they grow; they toil not, neither do they spin:

Matthew 21:21-22

Jesus answered and said unto them, Verily I say unto you, If ye have faith, and doubt not, ye shall not only do this which is done to the fig tree, but also if ye shall say unto this mountain, Be thou removed, and be thou cast into the sea; it shall be done. And all things, whatsoever ye shall ask in prayer, believing, ye shall receive.

Philip. 4:6

Be careful for nothing; but in every thing by prayer and supplication with thanksgiving let your requests be made known unto God.

PRAYER & SALVATION

Rev. Donald L. Bean, Jr.

"For I know that through your prayers and the help given by the Spirit of Jesus Christ, what has happened to me will turn out for my deliverance"

(Phil. 1:19, NIV).

Prayer is the work of the Church, and is an essential, spiritual discipline, needed for Salvation and quality, spiritual growth. The apostle Paul, facing multiple obstacles, heavy persecution, and imprisonment, relied upon prayer, turned to God, and trusted Him to turn his tragedy into triumph. This is prayer at its best. Paul relied on the prayers of the saints, believing that prayer, coupled with the work of the Holy Spirit, would trigger his dilemma to turn into deliverance (salvation).

Paul remained positive and even rejoiced while he was in prison going through his storm. Why? How did Paul endure hardships and still rejoice?

Paul's faith, hope, and trust in prayer allowed him to remain positive. Prayer, supported by strong faith, accomplishes more than our own power and strategies will ever accomplish. Surprisingly, many Christians consider using other methods first instead of relying on the power of prayer, and often use prayer as an add-on to the work of ministry instead of using prayer as the foundation for ministry. People praying together for the Salvation of lost souls are doing a very valuable work. This work may not be sexy, but it does have teeth. God has already supplied the provision for Salvation by sacrificing His Son. Prayer helps us engage and claim the power of Salvation.

PURPOSE

Matthew 6:33
But seek ye first the kingdom of God, and his righteousness; and all these things shall be added unto you.

Matthew 24:13
But he that shall endure unto the end, the same shall be saved.

2 Cor. 4:17
For our light affliction, which is but for a moment, worketh for us a far more exceeding and eternal weight of glory;

James 1:12
Blessed is the man that endureth temptation: for when he is tried, he shall receive the crown of life, which the Lord hath promised to them that love him.

Hebrews 12:1
Wherefore seeing we also are compassed about with so great a cloud of witnesses, let us lay aside every weight, and the sin which doth so easily beset us, and let us run with patience the race that is set before us,

Isaiah 43:18-19

Remember ye not the former things, neither consider the things of old. Behold, I will do a new thing; now it shall spring forth; shall ye not know it? I will even make a way in the wilderness, and rivers in the desert.

Ezekiel 34:16

I will seek that which was lost, and bring again that which was driven away, and will bind up that which was broken, and will strengthen that which was sick: but I will destroy the fat and the strong; I will feed them with judgment.

2 Cor. 5:17-18

Therefore if any man be in Christ, he is a new creature: old things are passed away; behold, all things are become new. And all things are of God, who hath reconciled us to himself by Jesus Christ, and hath given to us the ministry of reconciliation;

1 Peter 5:10

But the God of all grace, who hath called us unto his eternal glory by Christ Jesus, after that ye have suffered a while, make you perfect, stablish, strengthen, settle you.

Romans 7:24-25

O wretched man that I am! who shall deliver me from the body of this death? I thank God through Jesus Christ our Lord. So then with the mind I myself serve the law of God; but with the flesh the law of sin.

SALVATION

Romans 10:9-12

That if thou shalt confess with thy mouth the Lord Jesus, and shalt believe in thine heart that God hath raised him from the dead, thou shalt be saved. For with the heart man believeth unto righteousness; and with the mouth confession is made unto salvation. For the scripture saith, Whosoever believeth on him shall not be ashamed. For there is no difference between the Jew and the Greek: for the same Lord over all is rich unto all that call upon him.

Psalm 40:2

He brought me up also out of an horrible pit, out of the miry clay, and set my feet upon a rock, and established my goings.

Romans 3:23

For all have sinned, and come short of the glory of God;

1 Tim. 2:3-4

For this is good and acceptable in the sight of God our Saviour; Who will have all men to be saved, and to come unto the knowledge of the truth.

Titus 3:5

Not by works of righteousness which we have done, but according to his mercy he saved us, by the washing of regeneration, and renewing of the Holy Ghost;

SELF CONFIDENCE

Psalm 100:3

Know ye that the Lord he is God: it is he that hath made us, and not we ourselves; we are his people, and the sheep of his pasture.

Isaiah 49:15-16

Can a woman forget her sucking child, that she should not have compassion on the son of her womb? yea, they may forget, yet will I not forget thee. Behold, I have graven thee upon the palms of my hands; thy walls are continually before me.

Jeremiah 31:3

The Lord hath appeared of old unto me, saying, Yea, I have loved thee with an everlasting love: therefore with lovingkindness have I drawn thee.

Matthew 10:29-31

Are not two sparrows sold for a farthing? and one of them shall not fall on the ground without your Father. But the very hairs of your head are all numbered. Fear ye not therefore, ye are of more value than many sparrows.

Ephes. 1:5-6

Having predestinated us unto the adoption of children by Jesus Christ to himself, according to the good pleasure of his will, To the praise of the glory of his grace, wherein he hath made us accepted in the beloved.

SELF-CONTROL

Psalm 19:14
Let the words of my mouth, and the meditation of my heart, be acceptable in thy sight, O Lord, my strength, and my redeemer.

Galatians 5:22-23
But the fruit of the Spirit is love, joy, peace, longsuffering, gentleness, goodness, faith, Meekness, temperance: against such there is no law.

1 Tim. 4:7-8
But refuse profane and old wives' fables, and exercise thyself rather unto godliness. For bodily exercise profiteth little: but godliness is profitable unto all things, having promise of the life that now is, and of that which is to come.

Titus 2:4-5
That they may teach the young women to be sober, to love their husbands, to love their children, To be discreet, chaste, keepers at home, good, obedient to their own husbands, that the word of God be not blasphemed.

2 Peter 1:5-8
And beside this, giving all diligence, add to your faith virtue; and to virtue knowledge; And to knowledge temperance; and to temperance patience; and to patience godliness; And to godliness brotherly kindness; and to brotherly kindness charity. For if these things be in you, and abound, they make you that ye shall neither be barren nor unfruitful in the knowledge of our Lord Jesus Christ.

MINISTRY

George M. Matthews, II

What is this enigma called ministry? Many view it (ministry) as what ministers do as the message is presented during Sunday and midweek services. The truth, however, is that the word "ministry" is translated to mean, "servant." The word "servant" has incorporated in its meaning the idea of a bond slave—one who is under the total direction of his or her owner for work assignments, instructions, purpose, and lifestyle in general.

There is one thing about ministry to God that is different from the world's view of ministry: In serving Him, we become locked into servitude to mankind. Isaiah 55:8-9 states that God's method of doing things is "higher" than man's. When man thinks of ministry, he thinks of rising to a place of eminence or rulership, but God conceives a decreasing of the person involved in ministry so that His power, might, and ability may increase upon the individual (John 3:30).

SERVING

1 Chron. 28:9
 And thou, Solomon my son, know thou the God of thy father, and serve him with a perfect heart and with a willing mind: for the Lord searcheth all hearts, and understandeth all the imaginations of the thoughts: if thou seek him, he will be found of thee; but if thou forsake him, he will cast thee off for ever.

Luke 17:10
 So likewise ye, when ye shall have done all those things which are commanded you, say, We are unprofitable servants: we have done that which was our duty to do.

Romans 12:11
 Not slothful in business; fervent in spirit; serving the Lord;

John 15:12-17
 This is my commandment, That ye love one another, as I have loved you. Greater love hath no man than this, that a man lay down his life for his friends. Ye are my friends, if ye do whatsoever I command you. Henceforth I call you not servants; for the servant knoweth not what his lord doeth: but I have called you friends; for all things that I have heard of my Father I have made known unto you. Ye have not chosen me, but I have chosen you, and ordained you, that ye should go and bring forth fruit, and that your fruit should remain: that whatsoever ye shall ask of the Father in my name, he may give it you. These things I command you, that ye love one another.

SUFFERING

2 Cor. 4:7-9

But we have this treasure in earthen vessels, that the excellency of the power may be of God, and not of us. We are troubled on every side, yet not distressed; we are perplexed, but not in despair; Persecuted, but not forsaken; cast down, but not destroyed;

Psalm 33:22

Let thy mercy, O Lord, be upon us, according as we hope in thee.

Matthew 17:20

And Jesus said unto them, Because of your unbelief: for verily I say unto you, If ye have faith as a grain of mustard seed, ye shall say unto this mountain, Remove hence to yonder place; and it shall remove; and nothing shall be impossible unto you.

Romans 5:1

Therefore being justified by faith, we have peace with God through our Lord Jesus Christ:

1 Peter 1:21

Who by him do believe in God, that raised him up from the dead, and gave him glory; that your faith and hope might be in God.

TRUSTING

Psalm 102:27-28
But thou art the same, and thy years shall have no end. The children of thy servants shall continue, and their seed shall be established before thee.

Psalm 118:8
It is better to trust in the Lord than to put confidence in man.

Isaiah 26:3-4
Thou wilt keep him in perfect peace, whose mind is stayed on thee: because he trusteth in thee. Trust ye in the Lord for ever: for in the Lord Jehovah is everlasting strength:

Isaiah 30:15
For thus saith the Lord God, the Holy One of Israel; In returning and rest shall ye be saved; in quietness and in confidence shall be your strength: and ye would not.

Jeremiah 17:7-8
Blessed is the man that trusteth in the Lord, and whose hope the Lord is. For he shall be as a tree planted by the waters, and that spreadeth out her roots by the river, and shall not see when heat cometh, but her leaf shall be green; and shall not be careful in the year of drought, neither shall cease from yielding fruit.

WITNESSING

Psalm 126:6

He that goeth forth and weepeth, bearing precious seed, shall doubtless come again with rejoicing, bringing his sheaves with him.

Matthew 28:18-20

And Jesus came and spake unto them, saying, All power is given unto me in heaven and in earth. Go ye therefore, and teach all nations, baptizing them in the name of the Father, and of the Son, and of the Holy Ghost: Teaching them to observe all things whatsoever I have commanded you: and, lo, I am with you alway, even unto the end of the world. Amen.

Luke 10:2

Therefore said he unto them, The harvest truly is great, but the labourers are few: pray ye therefore the Lord of the harvest, that he would send forth labourers into his harvest.

John 4:39

And many of the Samaritans of that city believed on him for the saying of the woman, which testified, He told me all that ever I did.

Romans 10:9-10

That if thou shalt confess with thy mouth the Lord Jesus, and shalt believe in thine heart that God hath raised him from the dead, thou shalt be saved. For with the heart man believeth unto righteousness; and with the mouth confession is made unto salvation.

FAMILY/ PARENTING ISSUES

CHILDREN

Exodus 20:12
Honour thy father and thy mother: that thy days may be long upon the land which the Lord thy God giveth thee.

Proverbs 22:6
Train up a child in the way he should go: and when he is old, he will not depart from it.

Hebrews 12:10-11
For they verily for a few days chastened us after their own pleasure; but he for our profit, that we might be partakers of his holiness. Now no chastening for the present seemeth to be joyous, but grievous: nevertheless afterward it yieldeth the peaceable fruit of righteousness unto them which are exercised thereby.

Proverbs 19:18
Chasten thy son while there is hope, and let not thy soul spare for his crying.

Proverbs 29:15
The rod and reproof give wisdom: but a child left to himself bringeth his mother to shame.

DISCIPLINE

Dr. Arthur C. Banks

The only way our children will learn and commit to doing what is right is when rules are established, parameters are defined, consequences are established, and rewards and punishment are administered. The reason that many of our seniors and others are afraid to walk our streets is that many children are not disciplined to respect their elders or anyone else. Parents are relinquishing their parental authority because they are afraid of the child, and of governmental involvement if they discipline their child.

Parents must not let recent studies override our God-given mandate to "Train up a child in the way he should go: and when he is old, he will not depart from it" (Pro. 22:6). We must not allow anyone to frighten us away from training and disciplining our children.

DISCIPLINE

Deut. 8:5
Thou shalt also consider in thine heart, that, as a man chasteneth his son, so the Lord thy God chasteneth thee.

Proverbs 20:11
Even a child is known by his doings, whether his work be pure, and whether it be right.

Proverbs 29:17
Correct thy son, and he shall give thee rest; yea, he shall give delight unto thy soul.

Proverbs 13:24
He that spareth his rod hateth his son: but he that loveth him chasteneth him betimes.

3 John 1:4
I have no greater joy than to hear that my children walk in truth.

GIFT OF CHILDREN

Psalm 22:10
I was cast upon thee from the womb: thou art my God from my mother's belly.

Psalm 127:3-5
Lo, children are an heritage of the Lord: and the fruit of the womb is his reward. As arrows are in the hand of a mighty man; so are children of the youth. Happy is the man that hath his quiver full of them: they shall not be ashamed, but they shall speak with the enemies in the gate.

Matthew 10:42
And whosoever shall give to drink unto one of these little ones a cup of cold water only in the name of a disciple, verily I say unto you, he shall in no wise lose his reward.

Matthew 18:3
And said, Verily I say unto you, Except ye be converted, and become as little children, ye shall not enter into the kingdom of heaven.

Mark 10:14-16
But when Jesus saw it, he was much displeased, and said unto them, Suffer the little children to come unto me, and forbid them not: for of such is the kingdom of God. Verily I say unto you, Whosoever shall not receive the kingdom of God as a little child, he shall not enter therein. And he took them up in his arms, put his hands upon them, and blessed them.

GOD AS EXAMPLE

Deut. 6:4-7

Hear, O Israel: The Lord our God is one Lord: And thou shalt love the Lord thy God with all thine heart, and with all thy soul, and with all thy might. And these words, which command thee this day, shall be in thine heart: And thou shalt teach them diligently unto thy children, and shalt talk of them when thou sittest in thine house, and when thou walkest by the way, and when thou liest down, and when thou risest up.

Proverbs 19:18

Chasten thy son while there is hope, and let not thy soul spare for his crying.

Proverbs 22:6

Train up a child in the way he should go: and when he is old, he will not depart from it.

2 Cor. 6:18

And will be a Father unto you, and ye shall be my sons and daughters, saith the Lord Almighty.

Titus 2:1-6

But speak thou the things which become sound doctrine: That the aged men be sober, grave, temperate, sound in faith, in charity, in patience. The aged women likewise, that they be in behaviour as becometh holiness, not false accusers, not given to much wine, teachers of good things; That they may teach the young women to be sober, to love their husbands, to love their children, To be discreet, chaste, keepers at home, good, obedient to their own husbands, that the word of God be not blasphemed. Young men likewise exhort to be sober minded.

MARRIAGE

Ephes. 5:31-33
For this cause shall a man leave his father and mother, and shall be joined unto his wife, and they two shall be one flesh. This is a great mystery: but I speak concerning Christ and the church. Nevertheless let every one of you in particular so love his wife even as himself; and the wife see that she reverence her husband.

Eccles. 4:9-10
Two are better than one; because they have a good reward for their labour. For if they fall, the one will lift up his fellow: but woe to him that is alone when he falleth; for he hath not another to help him up.

Mark 10:8-9
And they twain shall be one flesh: so then they are no more twain, but one flesh. What therefore God hath joined together, let not man put asunder.

1 Cor. 7:4
The wife hath not power of her own body, but the husband: and likewise also the husband hath not power of his own body, but the wife.

THE VALUE OF FATHERHOOD

Dr. Jawanza Kunjufu

There is no greater gift that children could receive than love from their parents. Unfortunately, in the Black community, seventy percent of our children are living without their fathers. In my latest book, *State of Emergency: We Must Save African American Males*, I document that fatherlessness is a more significant indicator of social ills than race or income.

Fathers are more than breadwinners; they are the head of the family. Fathers are the priests of the house. They lead the family in prayer and teach the value of God's Word. These men are grounded in Joshua 24:15. When the family faces challenges, fathers use the kind of wisdom God gave Solomon to make godly decisions. Fathers are God's point people. When Eve ate the apple, God did not ask her first to explain her error. He went to Adam because God gave the instructions to the man.

There is a war between God and Satan for the man. In my earlier book, *Adam Where are You: Why Most Black Men Do Not Go To Church*, I gave twenty-one reasons to explain this unfortunate reality.

How can children believe in a heavenly daddy that they cannot see when their earthly daddy is MIA (missing in action)? The Lord reminds us in Malachi 4:6, "And he shall turn the heart of the fathers to the children, and the heart of the children to their fathers." Fathers need to turn their hearts to their children and be there for them, as their children turn their hearts to them.

RESPONSIBILITY OF PARENTING

Deut. 6:5-7

And thou shalt love the Lord thy God with all thine heart, and with all thy soul, and with all thy might. And these words, which I command thee this day, shall be in thine heart: And thou shalt teach them diligently unto thy children, and shalt talk of them when thou sittest in thine house, and when thou walkest by the way, and when thou liest down, and when thou risest up.

Joshua 24:15

And if it seem evil unto you to serve the Lord, choose you this day whom ye will serve; whether the gods which your fathers served that were on the other side of the flood, or the gods of the Amorites, in whose land ye dwell: but as for me and my house, we will serve the Lord.

Hebrews 12:9

Furthermore we have had fathers of our flesh which corrected us, and we gave them reverence: shall we not much rather be in subjection unto the Father of spirits, and live?

Matthew 18:3

And said, Verily I say unto you, Except ye be converted, and become as little children, ye shall not enter into the kingdom of heaven.

Ephes. 6:4

And, ye fathers, provoke not your children to wrath: but bring them up in the nurture and admonition of the Lord.

TEACHING CHILDREN

Psalm 71:6
   By thee have I been holden up from the womb: thou art he that took me out of my mother's bowels: my praise shall be continually of thee.

My hope for my children must be that they respond to the still, small voice of God in their own hearts.

Andrew Young

Psalm 78:5-7
   For he established a testimony in Jacob, and appointed a law in Israel, which he commanded our fathers, that they should make them known to their children: That the generation to come might know them, even the children which should be born; who should arise and declare them to their children: That they might set their hope in God, and not forget the works of God, but keep his commandments:

Psalm 139:13
   For thou hast possessed my reins: thou hast covered me in my mother's womb.

Mark 10:15
   Verily I say unto you, Whosoever shall not receive the kingdom of God as a little child, he shall not enter therein.

1 Tim. 4:12
   Let no man despise thy youth; but be thou an example of the believers, in word, in conversation, in charity, in spirit, in faith, in purity.

ATTRIBUTES OF GOD

AUTHORITY

Deut. 32:4

He is the Rock, his work is perfect: for all his ways are judgment: a God of truth and without iniquity, just and right is he.

Psalm 84:11

For the Lord God is a sun and shield: the Lord will give grace and glory: no good thing will he withhold from them that walk uprightly.

Psalm 33:11

The counsel of the Lord standeth for ever, the thoughts of his heart to all generations.

Jeremiah 29:11

For I know the thoughts that I think toward you, saith the Lord, thoughts of peace, and not of evil, to give you an expected end.

FORGIVENESS

Psalm 51:7

Purge me with hyssop, and I shall be clean: wash me, and I shall be whiter than snow.

Isaiah 44:22

I have blotted out, as a thick cloud, thy transgressions, and, as a cloud, thy sins: return unto me; for I have redeemed thee.

Joel 2:12-13

Therefore also now, saith the Lord, turn ye even to me with all your heart, and with fasting, and with weeping, and with mourning: And rend your heart, and not your garments, and turn unto the Lord your God: for he is gracious and merciful, slow to anger, and of great kindness, and repenteth him of the evil.

Col. 2:13-14

And you, being dead in your sins and the uncircumcision of your flesh, hath he quickened together with him, having forgiven you all trespasses; Blotting out the handwriting of ordinances that was against us, which was contrary to us, and took it out of the way, nailing it to his cross;

1 John 1:9

If we confess our sins, he is faithful and just to forgive us our sins, and to cleanse us from all unrighteousness.

HOLY

Psalm 46:10
Be still, and know that I am God: I will be exalted among the heathen, I will be exalted in the earth.

Psalm 100:3
Know ye that the Lord he is God: it is he that hath made us, and not we ourselves; we are his people, and the sheep of his pasture.

Isaiah 40:25
To whom then will ye liken me, or shall I be equal? saith the Holy One.

Jeremiah 23:23-24
Am I a God at hand, saith the Lord, and not a God afar off? Can any hide himself in secret places that I shall not see him? saith the Lord. Do not I fill heaven and earth? saith the Lord.

JUSTICE

Exodus 3:14

And God said unto Moses, I AM THAT I AM: and he said, Thus shalt thou say unto the children of Israel, I AM hath sent me unto you.

Exodus 34:6-7

And the Lord passed by before him, and proclaimed, The Lord, The Lord God, merciful and gracious, longsuffering, and abundant in goodness and truth, Keeping mercy for thousands, forgiving iniquity and transgression and sin, and that will by no means clear the guilty; visiting the iniquity of the fathers upon the children, and upon the children's children, unto the third and to the fourth generation.

Deut. 32:4

He is the Rock, his work is perfect: for all his ways are judgment: a God of truth and without iniquity, just and right is he.

Psalm 11:7

For the righteous Lord loveth righteousness; his countenance doth behold the upright.

Isaiah 30:18

And therefore will the Lord wait, that he may be gracious unto you, and therefore will he be exalted, that he may have mercy upon you: for the Lord is a God of judgment: blessed are all they that wait for him.

LOVE
Pastor Philip L. Rodman

Love. It is one of the most overused words in society, even in the church. We use "love" to describe how we feel about chocolate ice cream, the car, our careers, and even the family pet. The word has become such a cliche that it has lost its depth of meaning for us.

Part of the problem is that we really do not understand the meaning of love. Love is not a *feeling*. It is a *decision* that everyone must make. The Bible says that love, "bears all things, believes all things, hopes all things, endures all things" (1 Cor. 13:7, NKJV). Although people may not seem loveable to us, we can *decide* to love folk, just the same. We can put ourselves in their places and give them the highest love—that which Jesus Christ has given to us. Jesus says, "A new commandment I give unto you, That ye love one another; as I have loved you, that ye also love one another. By this shall all men know that ye are my disciples, if ye have love one to another" (John 13:34-35).

God never intended His people to become stagnant in their love toward others. However, Jesus says that in the last days, "And then shall many be offended, and shall betray one another, and shall hate one another. And because iniquity shall abound, the love of many shall wax cold" (Matt. 24:10,12).

As men of God and believers in Jesus Christ, we want to obey God and give others His love, even when we do not *feel* that they deserve love. After all, if Jesus Christ can love us, we can certainly love others, no matter how we may feel about them. This commandment is still worth obeying today!

LOVE

Psalm 16:11
Thou wilt shew me the path of life: in thy presence is fulness of joy; at thy right hand there are pleasures for evermore.

Psalm 33:18
Behold, the eye of the Lord is upon them that fear him, upon them that hope in his mercy;

Psalm 145:8
The Lord is gracious, and full of compassion; slow to anger, and of great mercy.

Ephes. 2:4-5
But God, who is rich in mercy, for his great love wherewith he loved us, Even when we were dead in sins, hath quickened us together with Christ, (by grace ye are saved;)

Philip. 1:6
Being confident of this very thing, that he which hath begun a good work in you will perform it until the day of Jesus Christ:

MERCY

Psalm 23:6
Surely goodness and mercy shall follow me all the days of my life: and I will dwell in the house of the Lord for ever.

Psalm 145:8
The Lord is gracious, and full of compassion; slow to anger, and of great mercy.

Titus 3:5
Not by works of righteousness which we have done, but according to his mercy he saved us, by the washing of regeneration, and renewing of the Holy Ghost;

James 5:11
Behold, we count them happy which endure. Ye have heard of the patience of Job, and have seen the end of the Lord; that the Lord is very pitiful, and of tender mercy.

1 Peter 1:3
Blessed be the God and Father of our Lord Jesus Christ, which according to his abundant mercy hath begotten us again unto a lively hope by the resurrection of Jesus Christ from the dead,

OMNISCIENCE

1 Samuel 16:7

But the Lord said unto Samuel, Look not on his countenance, or on the height of his stature; because I have refused him: for the Lord seeth not as man seeth; for man looketh on the outward appearance, but the Lord looketh on the heart.

Psalm 16:5

The Lord is the portion of mine inheritance and of my cup: thou maintainest my lot.

Psalm 33:13-15

The Lord looketh from heaven; he beholdeth all the sons of men. From the place of his habitation he looketh upon all the inhabitants of the earth. He fashioneth their hearts alike; he considereth all their works.

Isaiah 46:9-10

Remember the former things of old: for I am God, and there is none else; I am God, and there is none like me, Declaring the end from the beginning, and from ancient times the things that are not yet done, saying, My counsel shall stand, and I will do all my pleasure:

Romans 11:33

O the depth of the riches both of the wisdom and knowledge of God! how unsearchable are his judgments, and his ways past finding out!

PATIENCE

Psalm 86:15
But thou, O Lord, art a God full of compassion, and gracious, longsuffering, and plenteous in mercy and truth.

Psalm 130:5-6
I wait for the Lord, my soul doth wait, and in his word do I hope. My soul waiteth for the Lord more than they that watch for the morning: I say, more than they that watch for the morning.

1 Cor. 13:4-7
Charity suffereth long, and is kind; charity envieth not; charity vaunteth not itself, is not puffed up, Doth not behave itself unseemly, seeketh not her own, is not easily provoked, thinketh no evil; Rejoiceth not in iniquity, but rejoiceth in the truth; Beareth all things, believeth all things, hopeth all things, endureth all things.

Romans 12:12
Rejoicing in hope; patient in tribulation; continuing instant in prayer;

Col. 3:13
Forbearing one another, and forgiving one another, if any man have a quarrel against any: even as Christ forgave you, so also do ye.

PRESENCE

Psalm 42:8
   Yet the Lord will command his lovingkindness in the daytime, and in the night his song shall be with me, and my prayer unto the God of my life.

Isaiah 54:10
   For the mountains shall depart, and the hills be removed; but my kindness shall not depart from thee, neither shall the covenant of my peace be removed, saith the Lord that hath mercy on thee.

Lament. 3:22-23
   It is of the Lord's mercies that we are not consumed, because his compassions fail not. They are new every morning: great is thy faithfulness.

Isaiah 41:10
   Fear thou not; for I am with thee: be not dismayed; for I am thy God: I will strengthen thee; yea, I will help thee; yea, I will uphold thee with the right hand of my righteousness.

Isaiah 43:2-5

When thou passest through the waters, I will be with thee; and through the rivers, they shall not overflow thee: when thou walkest through the fire, thou shalt not be burned; neither shall the flame kindle upon thee. For I am the Lord thy God, the Holy One of Israel, thy Saviour:

I gave Egypt for thy ransom, Ethiopia and Seba for thee. Since thou wast precious in my sight, thou hast been honourable, and I have loved thee: therefore will I give men for thee, and people for thy life. Fear not: for I am with thee: I will bring thy seed from the east, and gather thee from the west.

PROVISION

Psalm 34:4
I sought the Lord, and he heard me, and delivered me from all my fears.

Isaiah 58:11
And the Lord shall guide thee continually, and satisfy thy soul in drought, and make fat thy bones: and thou shalt be like a watered garden, and like a spring of water, whose waters fail not.

Matthew 6:30-32
Wherefore, if God so clothe the grass of the field, which to day is, and to morrow is cast into the oven, shall he not much more clothe you, O ye of little faith? Therefore take no thought, saying, What shall we eat? or, What shall we drink? or, Wherewithal shall we be clothed? (For after all these things do the Gentiles seek:) for your heavenly Father knoweth that ye have need of all these things.

2 Cor. 9:8
And God is able to make all grace abound toward you; that ye, always having all sufficiency in all things, may abound to every good work:

Philip. 4:19
But my God shall supply all your need according to his riches in glory by Christ Jesus.

PROTECTION

Psalm 51:10-13

Create in me a clean heart, O God; and renew a right spirit within me. Cast me not away from thy presence; and take not thy holy spirit from me. Restore unto me the joy of thy salvation; and uphold me with thy free spirit. Then will I teach transgressors thy ways; and sinners shall be converted unto thee.

Psalm 55:22

Cast thy burden upon the Lord, and he shall sustain thee: he shall never suffer the righteous to be moved.

Psalm 91:14-15

Because he hath set his love upon me, therefore will I deliver him: I will set him on high, because he hath known my name. He shall call upon me, and I will answer him: I will be with him in trouble; I will deliver him, and honour him.

Romans 8:28

And we know that all things work together for good to them that love God, to them who are the called according to his purpose.

2 Cor. 1:3-4

Blessed be God, even the Father of our Lord Jesus Christ, the Father of mercies, and the God of all comfort; Who comforteth us in all our tribulation, that we may be able to comfort them which are in any trouble, by the comfort wherewith we ourselves are comforted of God.

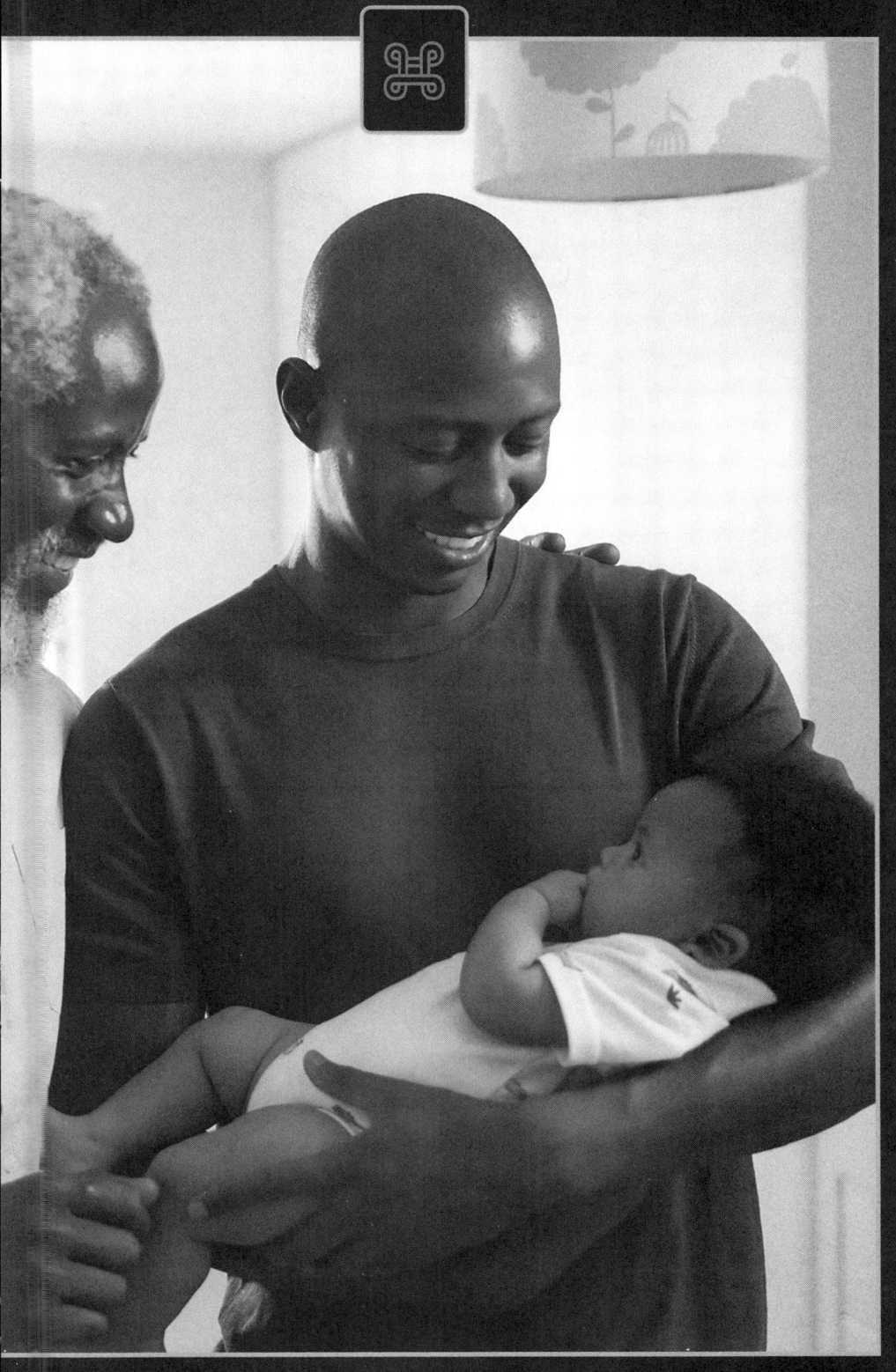

RIGHTEOUSNESS

Psalm 11:7
For the righteous Lord loveth righteousness; his countenance doth behold the upright.

Psalm 116:5
Gracious is the Lord, and righteous; yea, our God is merciful.

Romans 3:22
Even the righteousness of God which is by faith of Jesus Christ unto all and upon all them that believe: for there is no difference:

1 Cor. 1:30
But of him are ye in Christ Jesus, who of God is made unto us wisdom, and righteousness, and sanctification, and redemption:

2 Cor. 5:21
For he hath made him to be sin for us, who knew no sin; that we might be made the righteousness of God in him.

SOVEREIGNTY

1 Tim. 6:15-16
Which in his times he shall shew, who is the blessed and only Potentate, the King of kings, and Lord of lords; Who only hath immortality, dwelling in the light which no man can approach unto; whom no man hath seen, nor can see: to whom be honour and power everlasting. Amen.

Deut. 6:13-14
Thou shalt fear the Lord thy God, and serve him, and shalt swear by his name. Ye shall not go after other gods, of the gods of the people which are round about you;

1 Chron. 16:25
For great is the Lord, and greatly to be praised: he also is to be feared above all gods.

Psalm 66:3-4
Say unto God, How terrible art thou in thy works! through the greatness of thy power shall thine enemies submit themselves unto thee. All the earth shall worship thee, and shall sing unto thee; they shall sing to thy name. Selah.

Psalm 95:6-7
O come, let us worship and bow down: let us kneel before the Lord our maker. For he is our God; and we are the people of his pasture, and the sheep of his hand. To day if ye will hear his voice.

TRUTH

Exodus 34:6

And the Lord passed by before him, and proclaimed, The Lord, The Lord God, merciful and gracious, longsuffering, and abundant in goodness and truth,

Psalm 119:137

Righteous art thou, O Lord, and upright are thy judgments.

Psalm 145:17

The Lord is righteous in all his ways, and holy in all his works.

Jeremiah 23:5

Behold, the days come, saith the Lord, that I will raise unto David a righteous Branch, and a King shall reign and prosper, and shall execute judgment and justice in the earth.

Psalm 115:1-3

Not unto us, O Lord, not unto us, but unto thy name give glory, for thy mercy, and for thy truth's sake. Wherefore should the heathen say, Where is now their God? But our God is in the heavens: he hath done whatsoever he hath pleased.

RELATIONSHIP ISSUES

AGING

Eccles. 3:1
To every thing there is a season, and a time to every purpose under the heaven:

Proverbs 16:31
The hoary head is a crown of glory, if it be found in the way of righteousness.

Proverbs 31:30
Favour is deceitful, and beauty is vain: but a woman that feareth the Lord, she shall be praised.

Isaiah 61:10
I will greatly rejoice in the Lord, my soul shall be joyful in my God; for he hath clothed me with the garments of salvation, he hath covered me with the robe of righteousness, as a bridegroom decketh himself with ornaments, and as a bride adorneth herself with her jewels.

1 Peter 3:4
But let it be the hidden man of the heart, in that which is not corruptible, even the ornament of a meek and quiet spirit, which is in the sight of God of great price.

> "Age is a case of mind over matter.
> If you don't mind, it don't matter."
>
> Satchel Paige

COMMUNITY

Matthew 5:44-45

But I say unto you, Love your enemies, bless them that curse you, do good to them that hate you, and pray for them which despitefully use you, and persecute you; That ye may be the children of your Father which is in heaven: for he maketh his sun to rise on the evil and on the good, and sendeth rain on the just and on the unjust.

Luke 6:31

And as ye would that men should do to you, do ye also to them likewise.

Romans 14:19

Let us therefore follow after the things which make for peace, and things wherewith one may edify another.

Col. 3:12

Put on therefore, as the elect of God, holy and beloved, bowels of mercies, kindness, humbleness of mind, meekness, longsuffering;

James 2:8

If ye fulfil the royal law according to the scripture, Thou shalt love thy neighbour as thyself, ye do well:

ELDERLY

Psalm 71:17-18

O God, thou hast taught me from my youth: and hitherto have I declared thy wondrous works. Now also when I am old and greyheaded, O God, forsake me not; until I have shewed thy strength unto this generation, and thy power to every one that is to come.

Psalm 92:12-15

The righteous shall flourish like the palm tree: he shall grow like a cedar in Lebanon. Those that be planted in the house of the Lord shall flourish in the courts of our God. They shall still bring forth fruit in old age; they shall be fat and flourishing; To shew that the Lord is upright: he is my rock, and there is no unrighteousness in him.

Eccles. 3:22

Wherefore I perceive that there is nothing better, than that a man should rejoice in his own works; for that is his portion: for who shall bring him to see what shall be after him?

Isaiah 46:4

And even to your old age I am he; and even to hoar hairs will I carry you: I have made, and I will bear; even I will carry, and will deliver you.

Isaiah 52:7

How beautiful upon the mountains are the feet of him that bringeth good tidings, that publisheth peace; that bringeth good tidings of good, that publisheth salvation; that saith unto Zion, Thy God reigneth!

FRIENDSHIP

Jeremiah A. Wright, Jr.

Lord, He who thou loveth is sick…

The gift of friendship is one of the most precious gifts God gives us. A friend is a person who knows you "off stage." A friend knows your strengths and your weaknesses and yet loves you anyhow!

A friend is not judgmental; but a friend is also a person who will point out to you when and where you need to check yourself and change your behavior.

African-American men find it hard to form genuine friendships because we are always supposed to be "on stage." We have to keep up our "front." We have to "represent" and we have to maintain a "cool pose."

We erect our elaborate facades, therefore, we find it hard to take off the masks, be vulnerable, and let another black man know who we really are beneath the surface.

Jesus, however, shows us how to do just that. Jesus had a close friend in Lazarus of Bethany. Jesus loved Lazarus. Jesus could "chill" at Lazarus' home (see John 12:1-3).

Lazarus was known as the one "whom Jesus loved" (see John 11:4-6). Who holds that position in your life? Or are you afraid to be like Jesus?

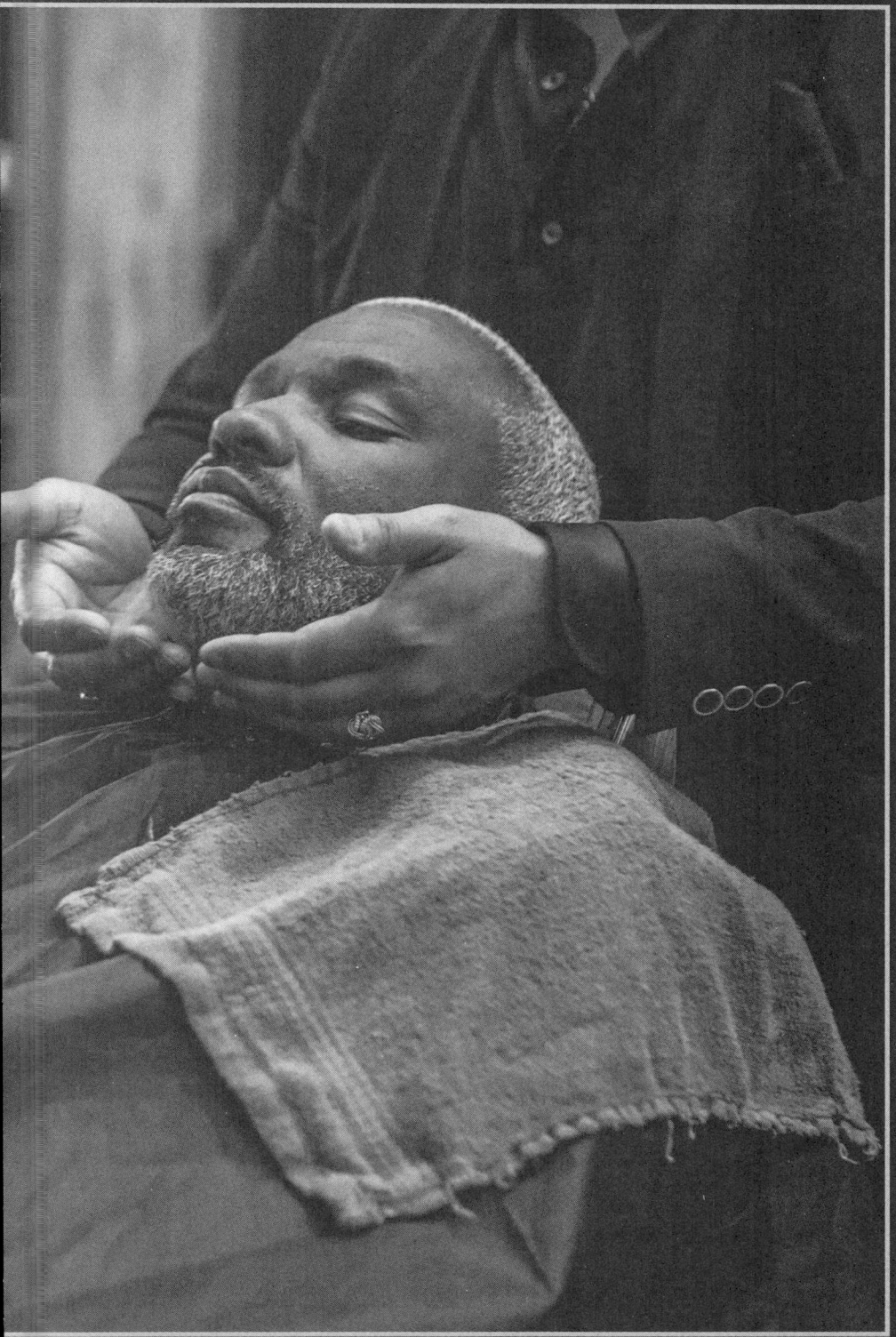

FRIENDSHIP

John 15:13
Greater love hath no man than this, that a man lay down his life for his friends.

Proverbs 17:19
He loveth transgression that loveth strife: and he that exalteth his gate seeketh destruction.

Proverbs 27:17
Iron sharpeneth iron; so a man sharpeneth the countenance of his friend.

Matthew 18:20
For where two or three are gathered together in my name, there am I in the midst of them.

John 13:14-15
If I then, your Lord and Master, have washed your feet; ye also ought to wash one another's feet. For I have given you an example, that ye should do as I have done to you.

INTIMACY WITH OTHERS

Jeremiah A. Wright, Jr.

"The one who leaned on Jesus' breast …"

John, the beloved disciple, was a godly, intimate companion of our Lord and Savior. Jesus could share his innermost human self—what Howard Thurman calls in us, "the nerve center of consent"—with John, and not experience rejection or misunderstanding.

Many African-American men have a problem with this type of godly, emotional intimacy. We are afraid to share our innermost selves with other men, as Jesus did. Likewise, we are afraid to share our innermost selves with women—even our mates who are life partners!

As the old saying in the Black community puts it: "If you ask a Black man *how* he is doing, he will tell you *what* he is doing!"

Being intimate means sharing our dreams, our hopes, our joys, our fears, our hurts, and our need for help. Most Black men cannot do that.

Jesus, however, demonstrated that He who was, "tough enough to die was also tender enough to cry!" When Jesus was in psychological pain over Judas's betrayal of Him, His intimate friend, John, asked who was causing the pain. Jesus answered him!

On the Cross of Calvary, Jesus asked His intimate friend to take care of His mother, Mary.

Being a follower of Jesus means no longer being afraid of intimacy. It means following the Lord's example and opening yourself up to be known, and to be loved in spite of your faults.

Dare to be Christ-like and dare to be intimate.

LOVE FOR OTHERS

Philip. 2:3-4

Let nothing be done through strife or vainglory; but in lowliness of mind let each esteem other better than themselves. Look not every man on his own things, but every man also on the things of others.

1 Peter 4:8

And above all things have fervent charity among yourselves: for charity shall cover the multitude of sins.

1 John 4:12

No man hath seen God at any time. If we love one another, God dwelleth in us, and his love is perfected in us.

1 John 3:16-18

Hereby perceive we the love of God, because he laid down his life for us: and we ought to lay down our lives for the brethren. But whoso hath this world's good, and seeth his brother have need, and shutteth up his bowels of compassion from him, how dwelleth the love of God in him? My little children, let us not love in word, neither in tongue; but in deed and in truth.

1 John 4:19

We love him, because he first loved us.

RESTORATION

Psalm 122:6-9

Pray for the peace of Jerusalem: they shall prosper that love thee. Peace be within thy walls, and prosperity within thy palaces. For my brethren and companions' sakes, I will now say, Peace be within thee. Because of the house of the Lord our God I will seek thy good.

Psalm 133:1

Behold, how good and how pleasant it is for brethren to dwell together in unity!

Ephes. 4:11-13

And he gave some, apostles; and some, prophets; and some, evangelists; and some, pastors and teachers; For the perfecting of the saints, for the work of the ministry, for the edifying of the body of Christ: Till we all come in the unity of the faith, and of the knowledge of the Son of God, unto a perfect man, unto the measure of the stature of the fulness of Christ:

Col. 2:2
   That their hearts might be comforted, being knit together in love, and unto all riches of the full assurance of understanding, to the acknowledgement of the mystery of God, and of the Father, and of Christ;

1 Peter 4:10
   As every man hath received the gift, even so minister the same one to another, as good stewards of the manifold grace of God.

Job 16:20

My friends scorn me: but mine eye poureth out tears unto God.

Proverbs 17:17

A friend loveth at all times, and a brother is born for adversity.

Proverbs 18:24

A man that hath friends must shew himself friendly: and there is a friend that sticketh closer than a brother.

Eccles. 4:9-12

Two are better than one; because they have a good reward for their labour. For if they fall, the one will lift up his fellow: but woe to him that is alone when he falleth; for he hath not another to help him up. Again, if two lie together, then they have heat: but how can one be warm alone? And if one prevail against him, two shall withstand him; and a threefold cord is not quickly broken.

Philip. 2:1-4

If there be therefore any consolation in Christ, if any comfort of love, if any fellowship of the Spirit, if any bowels and mercies, Fulfil ye my joy, that ye be likeminded, having the same love, being of one accord, of one mind. Let nothing be done through strife or vainglory; but in lowliness of mind let each esteem other better than themselves. Look not every man on his own things, but every man also on the things of others.

UNITY OF BELIEVERS

2 Cor. 13:11
Finally, brethren, farewell. Be perfect, be of good comfort, be of one mind, live in peace; and the God of love and peace shall be with you.

Galatians 3:28
There is neither Jew nor Greek, there is neither bond nor free, there is neither male nor female: for ye are all one in Christ Jesus.

Ephes. 4:4-6
There is one body, and one Spirit, even as ye are called in one hope of your calling; One Lord, one faith, one baptism, One God and Father of all, who is above all, and through all, and in you all.

1 Peter 1:22
Seeing ye have purified your souls in obeying the truth through the Spirit unto unfeigned love of the brethren, see that ye love one another with a pure heart fervently:

WHAT THE BIBLE SAYS ABOUT:

ANGER

Proverbs 16:1-3
The preparations of the heart in man, and the answer of the tongue, is from the Lord. All the ways of a man are clean in his own eyes; but the Lord weigheth the spirits. Commit thy works unto the Lord, and thy thoughts shall be established.

Galatians 5:24-26
And they that are Christ's have crucified the flesh with the affections and lusts. If we live in the Spirit, let us also walk in the Spirit. Let us not be desirous of vain glory, provoking one another, envying one another.

Galatians 6:9-10
And let us not be weary in well doing: for in due season we shall reap, if we faint not. As we have therefore opportunity, let us do good unto all men, especially unto them who are of the household of faith.

Ephes. 4:30-32
And grieve not the holy Spirit of God, whereby ye are sealed unto the day of redemption. Let all bitterness, and wrath, and anger, and clamour, and evil speaking, be put away from you, with all malice: And be ye kind one to another, tenderhearted, forgiving one another, even as God for Christ's sake hath forgiven you.

James 1:19-20
Wherefore, my beloved brethren, let every man be swift to hear, slow to speak, slow to wrath: For the wrath of man worketh not the righteousness of God.

BEAUTY

Genesis 1:26
And God said, Let us make man in our image, after our likeness: and let them have dominion over the fish of the sea, and over the fowl of the air, and over the cattle, and over all the earth, and over every creeping thing that creepeth upon the earth.

1 Samuel 16:7
But the Lord said unto Samuel, Look not on his countenance, or on the height of his stature; because I have refused him: for the Lord seeth not as man seeth; for man looketh on the outward appearance, but the Lord looketh on the heart.

Proverbs 31:30
Favour is deceitful, and beauty is vain: but a woman that feareth the Lord, she shall be praised.

Ephes. 4:22-24
That ye put off concerning the former conversation the old man, which is corrupt according to the deceitful lusts; And be renewed in the spirit of your mind; And that ye put on the new man, which after God is created in righteousness and true holiness.

Col. 3:12
Put on therefore, as the elect of God, holy and beloved, bowels of mercies, kindness, humbleness of mind, meekness, longsuffering;

BUSYNESS

Psalm 4:8

I will both lay me down in peace, and sleep: for thou, Lord, only makest me dwell in safety.

Proverbs 21:21

He that followeth after righteousness and mercy findeth life, righteousness, and honour.

Matthew 6:24

No man can serve two masters: for either he will hate the one, and love the other; or else he will hold to the one, and despise the other. Ye cannot serve God and mammon.

John 16:33

These things I have spoken unto you, that in me ye might have peace. In the world ye shall have tribulation: but be of good cheer; I have overcome the world.

Col. 3:15

And let the peace of God rule in your hearts, to the which also ye are called in one body; and be ye thankful.

POSITIVE THINKING

Floyd H. Flake

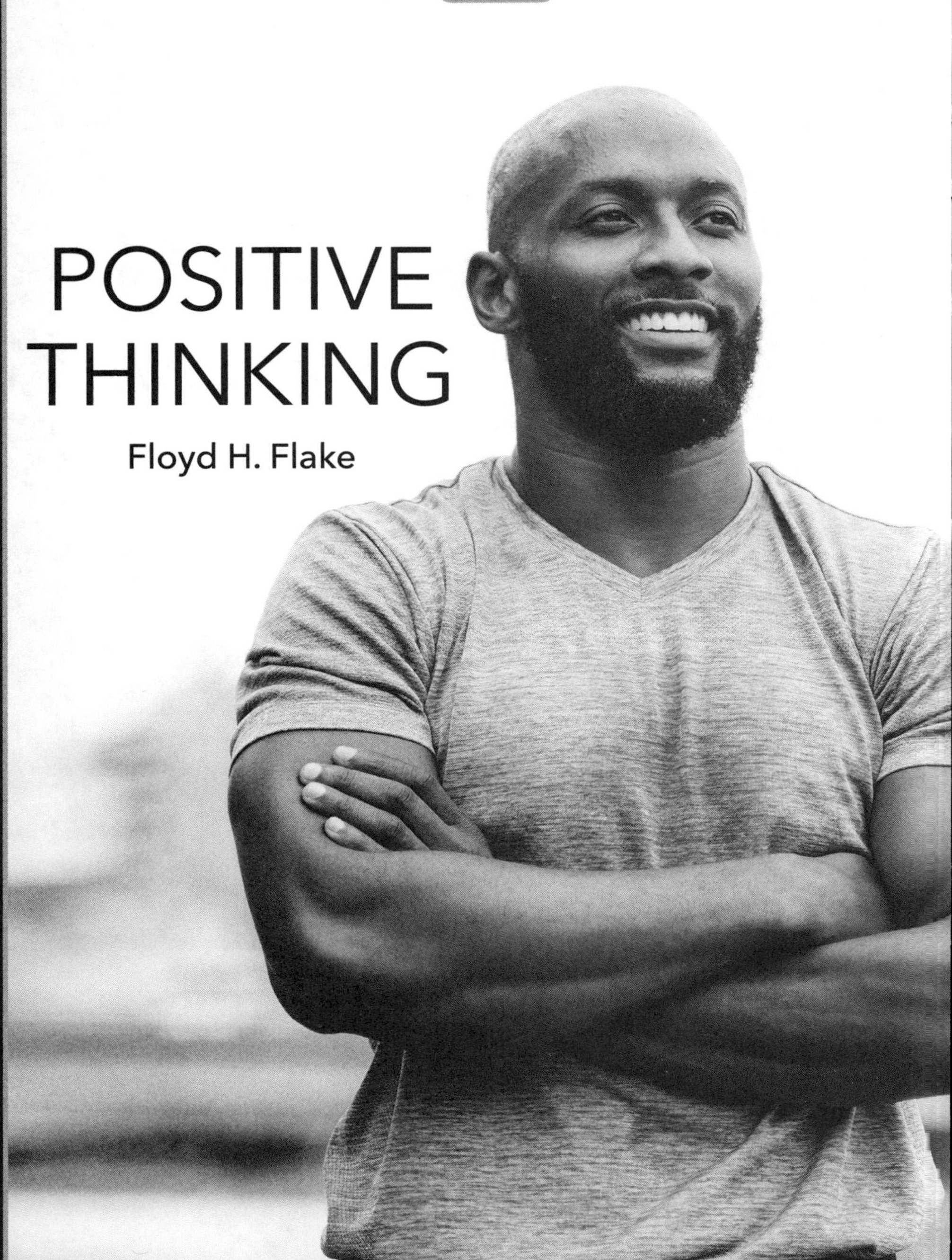

> *"Therefore I tell you, do not worry about your life, what you will eat or drink, or about your body, what you will wear."*
>
> Mathew 6:25a, NIV:

In the high-tech, paradigm-shifting, merger-manic, get-rich, quick-scheming, pressure-packed society that we live in, people are being driven to the edge of their wits by anxiety, worry, and fear for their future.

Many have developed negative means of coping; becoming cynical, jaded, losing faith in God. Others are guided by fears that keep them boxed and immobile. They are afraid to take risks, so they choose to do nothing—resulting in stagnant careers, broken relationships, inability to keep jobs, and having negative feelings about life.

Jesus commands us to stop being perpetually uneasy about life, worrying and being anxious about everything. Such feelings rob us of our joy, and make it impossible to appreciate the good things that God has provided for us. The Scripture challenges us to understand that God supplies our basic needs; therefore, there is no reason to worry.

Anxiety about little things keeps us from thinking positively and letting our "lights" shine in all situations. When we fail to think positively, the quality of our lives is negatively affected, causing unnecessary suffering and strife.

CONFIDENCE

Romans 11:33

O the depth of the riches both of the wisdom and knowledge of God! how unsearchable are his judgments, and his ways past finding out!

Psalm 18:32-33

It is God that girdeth me with strength, and maketh my way perfect. He maketh my feet like hinds' feet, and setteth me upon my high places.

Psalm 27:1

The Lord is my light and my salvation; whom shall I fear? the Lord is the strength of my life; of whom shall I be afraid?

Psalm 37:17-19

For the arms of the wicked shall be broken: but the Lord upholdeth the righteous. The Lord knoweth the days of the upright: and their inheritance shall be for ever. They shall not be ashamed in the evil time: and in the days of famine they shall be satisfied.

1 John 4:18-19

There is no fear in love; but perfect love casteth out fear: because fear hath torment. He that feareth is not made perfect in love. We love him, because he first loved us.

GIVING

Proverbs 28:27
He that giveth unto the poor shall not lack: but he that hideth his eyes shall have many a curse.

Luke 6:30
Give to every man that asketh of thee; and of him that taketh away thy goods ask them not again.

Luke 6:38
Give, and it shall be given unto you; good measure, pressed down, and shaken together, and running over, shall men give into your bosom. For with the same measure that ye mete withal it shall be measured to you again.

2 Cor. 9:6-7
But this I say, He which soweth sparingly shall reap also sparingly; and he which soweth bountifully shall reap also bountifully. Every man according as he purposeth in his heart, so let him give; not grudgingly, or of necessity: for God loveth a cheerful giver.

From what we get, we can make a living; what we give, however, makes a life.

Arthur Ashe

GUIDANCE

Psalm 86:8-10
Among the gods there is none like unto thee, O Lord; neither are there any works like unto thy works. All nations whom thou hast made shall come and worship before thee, O Lord; and shall glorify thy name. For thou art great, and doest wondrous things: thou art God alone.

Psalm 100:3
Know ye that the Lord he is God: it is he that hath made us, and not we ourselves; we are his people, and the sheep of his pasture.

Jeremiah 29:11
For I know the thoughts that I think toward you, saith the Lord, thoughts of peace, and not of evil, to give you an expected end.

Psalm 139:9-10
If I take the wings of the morning, and dwell in the uttermost parts of the sea; Even there shall thy hand lead me, and thy right hand shall hold me.

James 1:13
Let no man say when he is tempted, I am tempted of God: for God cannot be tempted with evil, neither tempteth he any man:

KNOWING GOD'S WILL

John 6:40

And this is the will of him that sent me, that every one which seeth the Son, and believeth on him, may have everlasting life: and I will raise him up at the last day.

Romans 12:2

And be not conformed to this world: but be ye transformed by the renewing of your mind, that ye may prove what is that good, and acceptable, and perfect, will of God.

Galatians 5:24

And they that are Christ's have crucified the flesh with the affections and lusts.

Ephes. 4:14-16

That we henceforth be no more children, tossed to and fro, and carried about with every wind of doctrine, by the sleight of men, and cunning craftiness, whereby they lie in wait to deceive; But speaking the truth in love, may grow up into him in all things, which is the head, even Christ: From whom the whole body fitly joined together and compacted by that which every joint supplieth, according to the effectual working in the measure of every part, maketh increase of the body unto the edifying of itself in love.

Philip. 3:20-21

For our conversation is in heaven; from whence also we look for the Saviour, the Lord Jesus Christ: Who shall change our vile body, that it may be fashioned like unto his glorious body, according to the working whereby he is able even to subdue all things unto himself.

LEADERSHIP:
Brick-By-Brick Together

George M. Matthews, II

As noted author John Maxwell said, "Leadership is the ability to attract followers." The absence of such results is one simply taking a walk in the park.

This premise statement indicates the strong correlation between leadership and followership. It is the followers who cause the vision of the leader to be implemented. The leader must possess the power to communicate the assignment clearly so that those who follow have an undivided sense of purpose.

This "brick" leads us to an understanding of what is spoken of in Habakkuk 2:2, "Write the vision, and make it plain upon tables, that he may run that readeth it." So we see the first and second components of leadership, revealing it to be a brick-by-brick, in-tandem relationship. The first component, obviously, is that of the leader making the vision plain or understandable.

The second is the "brick" of followers who receive this vision in its scope, who begin to embrace it and work in line with it because of their close association with the integral parts of it.

The final observation is winsome for all concerned parties, as the total "bricks" result in a completed project for all to admire.

LEADERSHIP

Joshua 24:15

And if it seem evil unto you to serve the Lord, choose you this day whom ye will serve; whether the gods which your fathers served that were on the other side of the flood, or the gods of the Amorites, in whose land ye dwell: but as for me and my house, we will serve the Lord.

John 15:16

Ye have not chosen me, but I have chosen you, and ordained you, that ye should go and bring forth fruit, and that your fruit should remain: that whatsoever ye shall ask of the Father in my name, he may give it you.

Proverbs 11:3

The integrity of the upright shall guide them: but the perverseness of transgressors shall destroy them.

Zech. 8:16

These are the things that ye shall do; Speak ye every man the truth to his neighbour; execute the judgment of truth and peace in your gates:

Ephes. 6:7

With good will doing service, as to the Lord, and not to men:

NATIONAL HERITAGE

Exodus 10:2
And that thou mayest tell in the ears of thy son, and of thy son's son, what things I have wrought in Egypt, and my signs which I have done among them; that ye may know how that I am the Lord.

Psalm 145:4
One generation shall praise thy works to another, and shall declare thy mighty acts.

Proverbs 20:7
The just man walketh in his integrity: his children are blessed after him.

Proverbs 22:6
Train up a child in the way he should go: and when he is old, he will not depart from it.

Psalm 78:4
We will not hide them from their children, shewing to the generation to come the praises of the Lord, and his strength, and his wonderful works that he hath done.

SECURITY

Psalm 68:6
God setteth the solitary in families: he bringeth out those which are bound with chains: but the rebellious dwell in a dry land.

Isaiah 54:5
For thy Maker is thine husband; the Lord of hosts is his name; and thy Redeemer the Holy One of Israel; The God of the whole earth shall he be called.

Isaiah 61:10
I will greatly rejoice in the Lord, my soul shall be joyful in my God; for he hath clothed me with the garments of salvation, he hath covered me with the robe of righteousness, as a bridegroom decketh himself with ornaments, and as a bride adorneth herself with her jewels.

Hosea 2:19-20
And I will betroth thee unto me for ever; yea, I will betroth thee unto me in righteousness, and in judgment, and in lovingkindness, and in mercies. I will even betroth thee unto me in faithfulness: and thou shalt know the Lord.

Matthew 28:20
Teaching them to observe all things whatsoever I have commanded you: and, lo, I am with you alway, even unto the end of the world. Amen.

SELF WORTH

Genesis 1:27

So God created man in his own image, in the image of God created he him; male and female created he them.

Deut. 14:2

for thou art an holy people unto the Lord thy God, and the Lord hath chosen thee to be a peculiar people unto himself, above all the nations that are upon the earth.

Jeremiah 1:5

Before I formed thee in the belly I knew thee; and before thou camest forth out of the womb I sanctified thee, and I ordained thee a prophet unto the nations.

Galatians 4:7

Wherefore thou art no more a servant, but a son; and if a son, then an heir of God through Christ.

John 3:16

For God so loved the world, that he gave his only begotten Son, that whosoever believeth in him should not perish, but have everlasting life.

SINGLENESS

1 Cor. 6:19-20
What? know ye not that your body is the temple of the Holy Ghost which is in you, which ye have of God, and ye are not your own? For ye are bought with a price: therefore glorify God in your body, and in your spirit, which are God's.

1 Cor. 7:34
There is difference also between a wife and a virgin. The unmarried woman careth for the things of the Lord, that she may be holy both in body and in spirit: but she that is married careth for the things of the world, how she may please her husband.

Psalm 73:23
Nevertheless I am continually with thee: thou hast holden me by my right hand.

1 Cor. 7:32
But I would have you without carefulness. He that is unmarried careth for the things that belong to the Lord, how he may please the Lord:

1 Peter 4:10
As every man hath received the gift, even so minister the same one to another, as good stewards of the manifold grace of God.

SINGLE LIFE

1 Peter 2:9

But ye are a chosen generation, a royal priesthood, an holy nation, a peculiar people; that ye should shew forth the praises of him who hath called you out of darkness into his marvellous light:

Genesis 2:18

And the Lord God said, It is not good that the man should be alone; I will make him an help meet for him.

Psalm 37:4-6

Delight thyself also in the Lord; and he shall give thee the desires of thine heart. Commit thy way unto the Lord; trust also in him; and he shall bring it to pass. And he shall bring forth thy righteousness as the light, and thy judgment as the noonday.

Matthew 6:33

But seek ye first the kingdom of God, and his righteousness; and all these things shall be added unto you.

Philip. 4:6

Be careful for nothing; but in every thing by prayer and supplication with thanksgiving let your requests be made known unto God.

Philip. 4:12

I know both how to be abased, and I know how to abound: every where and in all things I am instructed both to be full and to be hungry, both to abound and to suffer need.

SUFFERING

Psalm 46:10
Be still, and know that I am God: I will be exalted among the heathen, I will be exalted in the earth.

John 10:11
I am the good shepherd: the good shepherd giveth his life for the sheep.

Isaiah 54:10
For the mountains shall depart, and the hills be removed; but my kindness shall not depart from thee, neither shall the covenant of my peace be removed, saith the Lord that hath mercy on thee.

Lament. 3:22-23
It is of the Lord's mercies that we are not consumed, because his compassions fail not. They are new every morning: great is thy faithfulness.

Matthew 5:4-6
Blessed are they that mourn: for they shall be comforted. Blessed are the meek: for they shall inherit the earth. Blessed are they which do hunger and thirst after righteousness: for they shall be filled.

If there is no struggle, there is no progress.
Frederick Douglass

THOUGHTS

Romans 12:2

And be not conformed to this world: but be ye transformed by the renewing of your mind, that ye may prove what is that good, and acceptable, and perfect, will of God.

Philip. 4:13

I can do all things through Christ which strengtheneth me.

Proverbs 23:7

For as he thinketh in his heart, so is he: Eat and drink, saith he to thee; but his heart is not with thee.

Romans 8:6

For to be carnally minded is death; but to be spiritually minded is life and peace.

2 Cor. 10:5

Casting down imaginations, and every high thing that exalteth itself against the knowledge of God, and bringing into captivity every thought to the obedience of Christ;

TRUTH

Proverbs 23:23
Buy the truth, and sell it not; also wisdom, and instruction, and understanding.

John 8:32
And ye shall know the truth, and the truth shall make you free.

John 14:6
Jesus saith unto him, I am the way, the truth, and the life: no man cometh unto the Father, but by me.

John 16:13
Howbeit when he, the Spirit of truth, is come, he will guide you into all truth: for he shall not speak of himself; but whatsoever he shall hear, that shall he speak: and he will shew you things to come.

1 John 5:20
And we know that the Son of God is come, and hath given us an understanding, that we may know him that is true, and we are in him that is true, even in his Son Jesus Christ. This is the true God, and eternal life.

VANITY

1 Samuel 16:7

But the Lord said unto Samuel, Look not on his countenance, or on the height of his stature; because I have refused him: for the Lord seeth not as man seeth; for man looketh on the outward appearance, but the Lord looketh on the heart.

Proverbs 31:30

Favour is deceitful, and beauty is vain: but a woman that feareth the Lord, she shall be praised.

2 Cor. 3:18

But we all, with open face beholding as in a glass the glory of the Lord, are changed into the same image from glory to glory, even as by the Spirit of the Lord.

Ephes. 2:10

For we are his workmanship, created in Christ Jesus unto good works, which God hath before ordained that we should walk in them.

1 Peter 3:4

But let it be the hidden man of the heart, in that which is not corruptible, even the ornament of a meek and quiet spirit, which is in the sight of God of great price.

WORDS WE SAY

Romans 10:9-10
That if thou shalt confess with thy mouth the Lord Jesus, and shalt believe in thine heart that God hath raised him from the dead, thou shalt be saved. For with the heart man believeth unto righteousness; and with the mouth confession is made unto salvation.

Proverbs 15:4
A wholesome tongue is a tree of life: but perverseness therein is a breach in the spirit.

Ephes. 4:29
Let no corrupt communication proceed out of your mouth, but that which is good to the use of edifying, that it may minister grace unto the hearers.

James 3:2-3
For in many things we offend all. If any man offend not in word, the same is a perfect man, and able also to bridle the whole body. Behold, we put bits in the horses' mouths, that they may obey us; and we turn about their whole body.

1 Peter 4:11
If any man speak, let him speak as the oracles of God; if any man minister, let him do it as of the ability which God giveth: that God in all things may be glorified through Jesus Christ, to whom be praise and dominion for ever and ever. Amen.

TRIALS AND TROUBLES

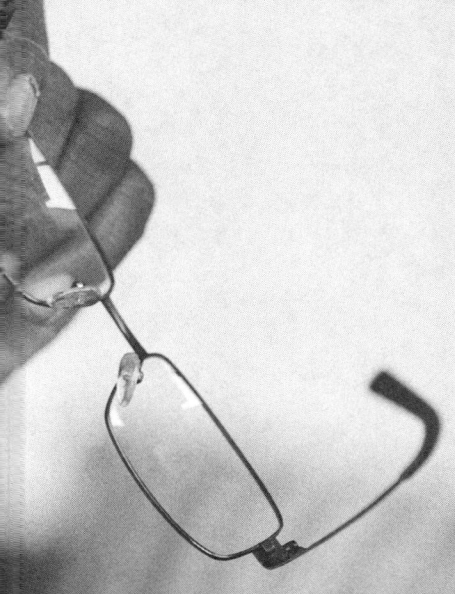

BROKENNESS

Psalm 34:18
The Lord is nigh unto them that are of a broken heart; and saveth such as be of a contrite spirit.

Psalm 51:7-11
Purge me with hyssop, and I shall be clean: wash me, and I shall be whiter than snow. Make me to hear joy and gladness; that the bones which thou hast broken may rejoice. Hide thy face from my sins, and blot out all mine iniquities. Create in me a clean heart, O God; and renew a right spirit within me. Cast me not away from thy presence; and take not thy holy spirit from me.

Psalm 118:8
It is better to trust in the Lord than to put confidence in man.

Proverbs 15:13
A merry heart maketh a cheerful countenance: but by sorrow of the heart the spirit is broken.

Mark 5:36
As soon as Jesus heard the word that was spoken, he saith unto the ruler of the synagogue, Be not afraid, only believe.

DEATH

2 Cor. 5:1
For we know that if our earthly house of this tabernacle were dissolved, we have a building of God, an house not made with hands, eternal in the heavens.

John 14:2
In my Father's house are many mansions: if it were not so, I would have told you. I go to prepare a place for you.

Philip. 3:20
For our conversation is in heaven; from whence also we look for the Saviour, the Lord Jesus Christ:

Rev. 7:16-17
They shall hunger no more, neither thirst any more; neither shall the sun light on them, nor any heat. For the Lamb which is in the midst of the throne shall feed them, and shall lead them unto living fountains of waters: and God shall wipe away all tears from their eyes.

Rev. 21:4
And God shall wipe away all tears from their eyes; and there shall be no more death, neither sorrow, nor crying, neither shall there be any more pain: for the former things are passed away.

DESPAIR

Psalm 118:6

The Lord is on my side; I will not fear: what can man do unto me?

Isaiah 41:10

Fear thou not; for I am with thee: be not dismayed; for I am thy God: I will strengthen thee; yea, I will help thee; yea, I will uphold thee with the right hand of my righteousness.

Matthew 10:30-31

But the very hairs of your head are all numbered. Fear ye not therefore, ye are of more value than many sparrows.

2 Cor. 12:9

And he said unto me, My grace is sufficient for thee: for my strength is made perfect in weakness. Most gladly therefore will I rather glory in my infirmities, that the power of Christ may rest upon me.

2 Thes. 2:16-17

Now our Lord Jesus Christ himself, and God, even our Father, which hath loved us, and hath given us everlasting consolation and good hope through grace, Comfort your hearts, and stablish you in every good word and work.

Hebrews 6:10

For God is not unrighteous to forget your work and labour of love, which ye have shewed toward his name, in that ye have ministered to the saints, and do minister.

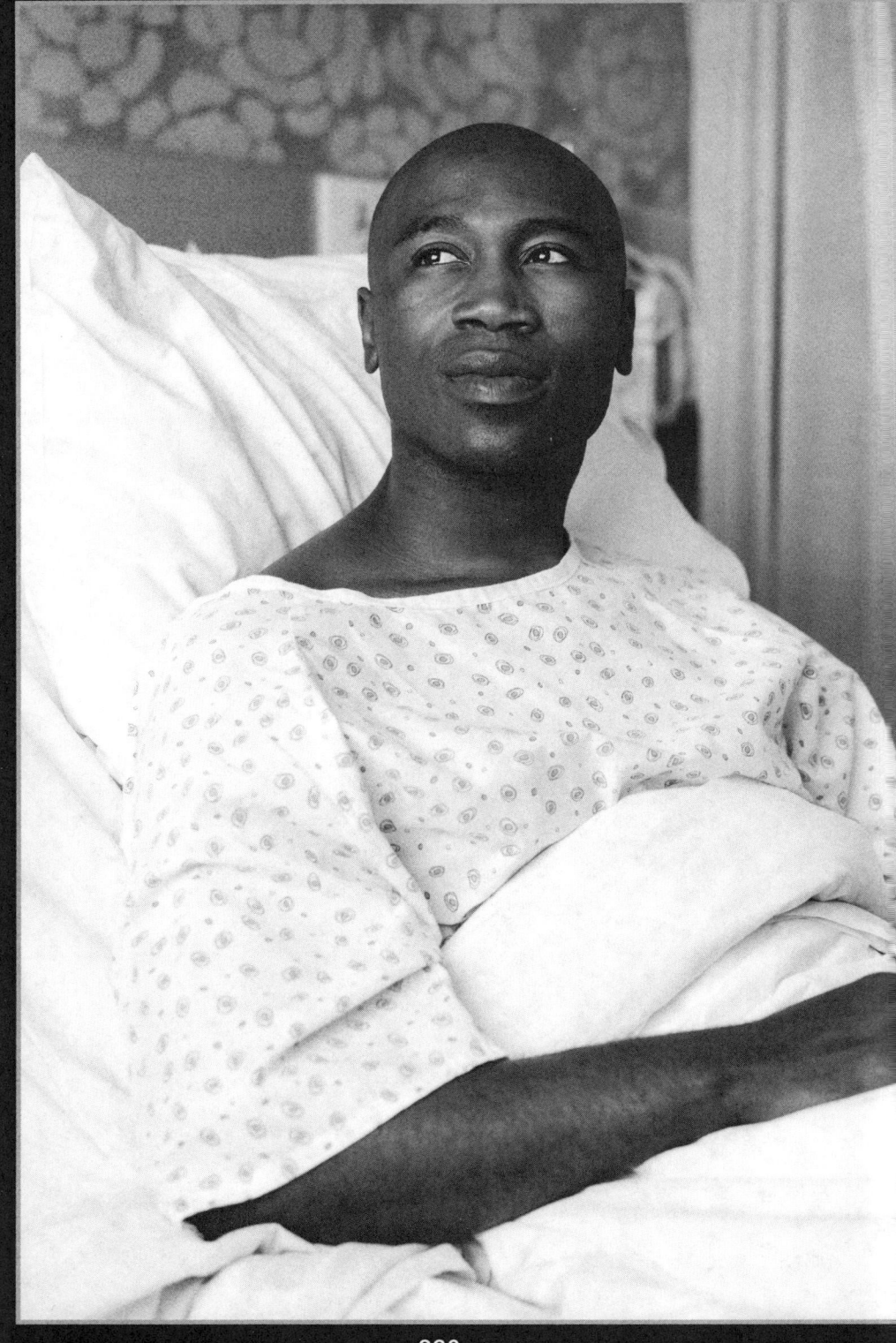

DISCOURAGEMENT

Psalm 43:5
Why art thou cast down, O my soul? and why art thou disquieted within me? hope in God: for I shall yet praise him, who is the health of my countenance, and my God.

Hebrews 6:10
For God is not unrighteous to forget your work and labour of love, which ye have shewed toward his name, in that ye have ministered to the saints, and do minister.

Mark 14:36
And he said, Abba, Father, all things are possible unto thee; take away this cup from me: nevertheless not what I will, but what thou wilt.

Philip. 4:6-7
Be careful for nothing; but in every thing by prayer and supplication with thanksgiving let your requests be made known unto God. And the peace of God, which passeth all understanding, shall keep your hearts and minds through Christ Jesus.

1 Thes. 5:16-18
Rejoice evermore. Pray without ceasing. In every thing give thanks: for this is the will of God in Christ Jesus concerning you.

> *God gives nothing to those who keep their arms crossed.*
> African Proverb

FEAR

Psalm 34:4-5

I sought the Lord, and he heard me, and delivered me from all my fears. They looked unto him, and were lightened: and their faces were not ashamed.

Psalm 18:32

It is God that girdeth me with strength, and maketh my way perfect.

Psalm 31:24

Be of good courage, and he shall strengthen your heart, all ye that hope in the Lord.

Isaiah 43:2-3

When thou passest through the waters, I will be with thee; and through the rivers, they shall not overflow thee: when thou walkest through the fire, thou shalt not be burned; neither shall the flame kindle upon thee. For I am the Lord thy God, the Holy One of Israel, thy Saviour: I gave Egypt for thy ransom, Ethiopia and Seba for thee.

Isaiah 50:7

For the Lord God will help me; therefore shall I not be confounded: therefore have I set my face like a flint, and I know that I shall not be ashamed.

GRIEF

Psalm 23:3-4

He restoreth my soul: he leadeth me in the paths of righteousness for his name's sake. Yea, though I walk through the valley of the shadow of death, I will fear no evil: for thou art with me; thy rod and thy staff they comfort me.

Psalm 55:17

Evening, and morning, and at noon, will I pray, and cry aloud: and he shall hear my voice.

Psalm 61:1-2

Hear my cry, O God; attend unto my prayer. From the end of the earth will I cry unto thee, when my heart is overwhelmed: lead me to the rock that is higher than I.

2 Cor. 4:14

Knowing that he which raised up the Lord Jesus shall raise up us also by Jesus, and shall present us with you.

1 Thes. 4:14

For if we believe that Jesus died and rose again, even so them also which sleep in Jesus will God bring with him.

LONELINESS

Psalm 46:10
Be still, and know that I am God: I will be exalted among the heathen, I will be exalted in the earth.

Psalm 145:18
The Lord is nigh unto all them that call upon him, to all that call upon him in truth.

Acts 17:27
That they should seek the Lord, if haply they might feel after him, and find him, though he be not far from every one of us:

Hebrews 13:5
Let your conversation be without covetousness; and be content with such things as ye have: for he hath said, I will never leave thee, nor forsake thee.

Mark 1:35
And in the morning, rising up a great while before day, he went out, and departed into a solitary place, and there prayed.

SORROW

Psalm 10:17
Lord, thou hast heard the desire of the humble: thou wilt prepare their heart, thou wilt cause thine ear to hear:

Psalm 34:18
The Lord is nigh unto them that are of a broken heart; and saveth such as be of a contrite spirit.

Jeremiah 31:13
Then shall the virgin rejoice in the dance, both young men and old together: for I will turn their mourning into joy, and will comfort them, and make them rejoice from their sorrow.

2 Cor. 1:3-4
Blessed be God, even the Father of our Lord Jesus Christ, the Father of mercies, and the God of all comfort; Who comforteth us in all our tribulation, that we may be able to comfort them which are in any trouble, by the comfort wherewith we ourselves are comforted of God.

Hebrews 4:14-16
Seeing then that we have a great high priest, that is passed into the heavens, Jesus the Son of God, let us hold fast our profession. For we have not an high priest which cannot be touched with the feeling of our infirmities; but was in all points tempted like as we are, yet without sin. Let us therefore come boldly unto the throne of grace, that we may obtain mercy, and find grace to help in time of need.

STRESS

Psalm 107:6-9

Then they cried unto the Lord in their trouble, and he delivered them out of their distresses. And he led them forth by the right way, that they might go to a city of habitation. Oh that men would praise the Lord for his goodness, and for his wonderful works to the children of men! For he satisfieth the longing soul, and filleth the hungry soul with goodness.

Psalm 18:16

He sent from above, he took me, he drew me out of many waters.

Psalm 30:11-12

Thou hast turned for me my mourning into dancing: thou hast put off my sackcloth, and girded me with gladness; To the end that my glory may sing praise to thee, and not be silent. O Lord my God, I will give thanks unto thee for ever.

Jeremiah 6:16

Thus saith the Lord, Stand ye in the ways, and see, and ask for the old paths, where is the good way, and walk therein, and ye shall find rest for your souls. But they said, We will not walk therein.

1 Thes. 5:18

In every thing give thanks: for this is the will of God in Christ Jesus concerning you.

TEMPTATION

Psalm 119:105
Thy word is a lamp unto my feet, and a light unto my path.

Matthew 26:41
Watch and pray, that ye enter not into temptation: the spirit indeed is willing, but the flesh is weak.

Titus 2:11-12
For the grace of God that bringeth salvation hath appeared to all men, Teaching us that, denying ungodliness and worldly lusts, we should live soberly, righteously, and godly, in this present world;

James 1:13-15
Let no man say when he is tempted, I am tempted of God: for God cannot be tempted with evil, neither tempteth he any man: But every man is tempted, when he is drawn away of his own lust, and enticed. Then when lust hath conceived, it bringeth forth sin: and sin, when it is finished, bringeth forth death.

James 4:7
Submit yourselves therefore to God. Resist the devil, and he will flee from you.

The time is always right to do what is right.
Reverend Dr. Martin Luther King, Jr., activist

TROUBLE

2 Cor. 4:16-18

For which cause we faint not; but though our outward man perish, yet the inward man is renewed day by day. For our light affliction, which is but for a moment, worketh for us a far more exceeding and eternal weight of glory; While we look not at the things which are seen, but at the things which are not seen: for the things which are seen are temporal; but the things which are not seen are eternal.

2 Cor. 12:9

And he said unto me, My grace is sufficient for thee: for my strength is made perfect in weakness. Most gladly therefore will I rather glory in my infirmities, that the power of Christ may rest upon me.

Philip. 1:6

Being confident of this very thing, that he which hath begun a good work in you will perform it until the day of Jesus Christ:

James 1:12

Blessed is the man that endureth temptation: for when he is tried, he shall receive the crown of life, which the Lord hath promised to them that love him.

POSITIVE THINKING

Willard Ashley Sr

What is positive thinking? Some attribute positive thinking to the late Norman Vincent Peale, pastor of the Marble Collegiate Church in New York City for fifty-two years. Others trace positive thinking back to the men and women of faith in the scriptures. Centuries before Dr. Martin Luther King, Jr., was born, Joseph had a dream. Shadrach, Meshach, and Abednego told King Nebuchadnezzar, "Our God is able to deliver us from your hand" (Daniel 3:17, KJV). Jesus stated, "Greater is he who is in you than he who is in the world" (1 John 4:4, KJV). Paul proclaimed, "I can do all things through Christ who strengths me" (Philippians 4:13, KJV).

Positive thinking is more than a gimmick or sound bite designed to boost one's self esteem. It is our confidence in the power of God to accomplish in us that which God sets out to do. Positive thinking is our ticket to dream, to develop to our full potential, to strive for excellence, to be optimists, and to make every day a good day. "This is the day that the Lord has made. We shall rejoice and be glad in it" (Psalm 118:24, KJV).

WORRY

Psalm 18:1-2

To the chief Musician, A Psalm of David, the servant of the Lord, who spake unto the Lord the words of this song in the day that the Lord delivered him from the hand of all his enemies, and from the hand of Saul: And he said,

I will love thee, O Lord, my strength. The Lord is my rock, and my fortress, and my deliverer; my God, my strength, in whom I will trust; my buckler, and the horn of my salvation, and my high tower.

Psalm 32:7

Thou art my hiding place; thou shalt preserve me from trouble; thou shalt compass me about with songs of deliverance. Selah.

Psalm 55:22

Cast thy burden upon the Lord, and he shall sustain thee: he shall never suffer the righteous to be moved.

Philip. 4:19

But my God shall supply all your need according to his riches in glory by Christ Jesus.

Matthew 6:25-28

Therefore I say unto you, Take no thought for your life, what ye shall eat, or what ye shall drink; nor yet for your body, what ye shall put on. Is not the life more than meat, and the body than raiment? Behold the fowls of the air: for they sow not, neither do they reap, nor gather into barns; yet your heavenly Father feedeth them. Are ye not much better than they? Which of you by taking thought can add one cubit unto his stature? And why take ye thought for raiment? Consider the lilies of the field, how they grow; they toil not, neither do they spin:

☑ GOALS

Become an US Urban Spirit! Publishing and Media Company Independent or Church Distributor Today!

- earn extra money
- engage with more people
- change lives
- join a winning team
- distribute high-quality Bibles and books

Go to www.urbanspirit.biz

Order your Independent or Church Distributor "Starter Kit" today online. It contains everything you need to get started selling right away.
Or call **800.560.1690** to get started today!